The Good News

Introducing the Historical Jesus and His Biographies

God's richest blessings to you,
brother Mike.

Copyright Statement

Rabboni Laboratories,
200, Mawney Road,
Romford - RM7 8BU.
United Kingdom.
www.rabboni-labs.com
email: info@rabboni-labs.com

ISBN: 978-0-9932945-1-8

Printed in India, 2017.

Dedication

I dedicate this work to my Lord, saviour, teacher, shepherd, brother and best friend, Jesus the Christ, who, being in the form of God, did not consider it robbery to be equal with God, but made Himself of no reputation, taking the form of a bondservant, and coming in the likeness of men and being found in appearance as a man, He humbled Himself and became obedient to the point of death, even the death of the cross [Philippians 2:6-8, The Bible] to redeem a wretch like me.

Arul Velusamy.

Table of Contents

List of Tables

List of Figures

Acknowledgements

First and foremost, I would like to thank God my Father and my Lord Jesus Christ, who have considered even a wretch like me, as a servant, to steward His Word.

Second, I would like to thank my entire family - Velusamy Karuppan, Margret Velusamy, Dr. Sudhagar Somasundaram, Dr. Sweetha Sudhagar Somasundaram, Sudeeth Ben Iniyan and Abishai Ben Amudhan who have been a great encouragement in my ministry to the LORD.

Third, I would like to thank Charlotte Saunders who agreed to review the manuscript for this book.

Fourth, I would like to thank my friends - Darren & Janett Lawrence and Ruby Kurian, who have been a constant support for me over the last many years

1. Introduction

Today, we would find claims, in Christian circles, that Jesus is God who took up flesh and blood like us, human beings, in order to vicariously die for us, to pay the penalty of our rebellion against God, and subsequently, to reconcile us back to God, after our wandering away from God, and rose again back to life and entered into the heavens, to give us hope of an eternal life. This, they would claim, we know, through scriptures, the Bible, and more accurately, the Gospels (biographies of Jesus) in the New Testament. There is only one catch here. That is, how do we know if this is true? After all, if Jesus is as important to us, as our saviour, as they make it out to be, then surely, we just could not depend on these claims merely because these claims exist, but rather, we would have to be convinced that there is a way to verify that the claims are true, and to subsequently verify the claims ourselves.

If we carefully dissect the claims corresponding to Jesus and the Gospels, we would identify that there are broadly 3 sub-claims that stare at us in our faces.

Firstly, that we somehow, rather audaciously, have documentary evidences (or any other evidence for that matter) of the happenings in first century Judea, Samaria, Galilee and Perea where Jesus is claimed to have lived, and had his early followers. How wonderful would it be, if we are able to establish that the Gospels themselves, which are purported to be the primary sources of information of Jesus, are close enough in time and space (and whatever else that may separate him from us today) to Jesus, and form part of this documentary evidences bounty. Once we establish this, we would then have a chance of seeing if the Gospels are reliable as documents of history, and thereby progressing further in our scrutiny. However, if we fail in establishing that the Gospels are close enough to Jesus, then we have a greatly reduced (in terms of confidence) opportunity in knowing about Jesus (even if there ever was such a person), because apart from the Gospels there isn't much in the form of primary sources of information concerning Jesus.

Secondly, that the documentary (and other kinds of) evidences that we establish to be close enough to Jesus, is verifiable to be historically reliable, and intended to be accurate out and out. What would be obvious is that, if we find that the Gospels are works of fiction, written in fantasy style and settings, then they would be of almost no use in getting to know about Jesus (even if he was historical), except in gleaning minor details related to cultural context of his time. However, what would be less obvious is that, if the Gospels are works of fiction, laid out in a historical setting, or works of history in fictional settings, they would be not very useful in getting to know about a possibly historical Jesus. In other words, if the Gospels were indeed proven to be close enough to Jesus, we would like to establish that the Gospels were intended to be works of history laid out in a historical setting, and were taken as such, to our relief, even by the supporters and critics who were close enough to Jesus, so that we could confidently use the Gospels in constructing a picture of a possibly historical Jesus.

Thirdly, that the picture of the historical Jesus is somehow clear enough, and that it could be construed as only to be that of someone who is divine, who died and rose again back to life, in a verifiable way. When exploring the Gospels after having established it to be historically reliable, to clear thinkers, nothing would be as prominent as questions ultimately related to Jesus' divinity. These questions may take various forms such as, "Did Jesus claim to be divine and did he prove it?", "Is the resurrection of Jesus true?" and "Did Jesus' contemporaries believe in his resurrection?" etc. Answer to the 'divinity question' would then dictate the tone of our conversation about anything else that Jesus said or did.

Enough has been said, by way of introduction. Now is time to dive deep and explore. Are the Gospels close enough to represent a possibly historical Jesus? Are the Gospels reliable documents of history? Is Jesus God?

2. Jesus and the Gospels - an Introduction

What used to be Israel sometime before the 1st century, and a bit more than what is again today Israel, was a divided land in the 1st century. The divisions, Judea, Samaria, Galilee and Perea like various other portions of the world, were under the Roman Emperor at that time, albeit 'ruled' or 'administered'/'governed' by local representatives of varying power. The primary people groups in that area were the Jews and the Samaritans. However, owing to the Roman occupation, and the lack of strict borders one would expect to find a reasonable number of Romans or people from the neighbouring regions like Syria, Phoenicia etc settled in that area. The world would have been reasonably open at that time, with a traveller from one of Judea, Samaria, Galilee and Perea having flexibility of travelling across a wider portion of the world, albeit not with as much comfort or speed as one would expect to have in his travel, today. Prominent religion of the land would have been Judaism, with institutions such as the Jerusalem Temple and Synagogues taking prominent places in the lives of people. Groups such as the Pharisees, Sadducees, Scribes, Elders, Chief Priests and High Priest would have wielded considerable influence over the lives of people, along with the Roman authorities. People in this region would have reasonably spoken or had at least an elementary proficiency to read and write in Greek (as the lingua franca), Hebrew and Aramaic (as native tongues) and Latin (owing to the Roman influence).

It was in this context, that Jesus was claimed to have lived, having born in Bethlehem near Jerusalem (near the close of the BC era, not so surprisingly) and having spent most of his adolescent life in Nazareth of Galilee. Of course, these statements about Jesus (and future statements in this introduction section about Jesus and the Gospels) are merely claims for us, at this stage, and we would be delighted to see if we are, in some way, able to verify the veracity of such claims, as we go through our scrutiny. However, it would be best to have some of these claims stated up front, so we have a rough context set, for our scrutiny of Jesus and the Gospels. He is believed to have started his public preaching and teaching around the age of 30, and to have picked up followers, over a little more than 3 years of such preaching and teaching. His public preaching is also claimed to have been accompanied with miracles such as healing lepers, blind and lame and even raising dead people back to life. For varying reasons, he is said to have picked up opposition from amongst Pharisees, Sadducees, Scribes, Elders, Chief Priests and the High Priest, during the course of his ministry. All the opposition seems to have culminated in some people in the Jewish leadership recommending, to the Roman prefect of Judea of that time, to have Jesus executed by crucifixion. If all had ended with the eventual crucifixion of Jesus, perhaps we might not have been exploring his life today. What then seems to have happened, according to those ardent followers of his, both of that time and today, was that he was dead, buried but later came back alive to be seen by them and/or to be interacting with them, and that he had required their continued allegiance in taking him to be God, and spreading news about his life and divinity, across the world, until he returns back once more in the future. Now you see why we are even exploring the life of Jesus and the Gospels - we are, in some way, forced to hear this news even today, by some of these ardent followers, namely Christians!

Now, about the Gospels, the word 'gospel' means 'good news'. Four works, which are claimed to be biographical works on Jesus, traditionally attributed to Matthew, Mark, Luke and John are called Gospels, as they, according to followers of Jesus, contain a certain 'good news' available in and through the life of Jesus. These four books are understood to be the primary literary sources of information for the life of the purported historical Jesus written originally in Greek (presumably with the intention of spreading the news far and wide, as Greek was the lingua franca of that time). These Gospels are part of a larger collection of documents called the New Testament, which Christians use as scriptures (documents sacred because of divine origin), along with the Hebrew Bible. Apart from the Gospels, the New Testament has other books (originally written in Greek) related to the history of the early disciples of Jesus i.e. the early church (Acts of the Apostles), various letters written to clarify teachings of Jesus (Pauline and catholic epistles) and a prophetic book (Revelation). Most, if not all of the New Testament, is said to have been completed by the turn of the century (1st century), mostly by contemporaries and eyewitnesses of Jesus.

3. Gospels - Do We Have Accurate 1st Century Text?[1]

To ask the question - 'Are the Gospels close enough to Jesus?' is roughly the same as asking 'Do we have accurate 1st century text of the Gospels?'

Since the invention of printing with movable type in the 15th century AD, there have been at least a few billion copies of the Gospels, printed and published in over a thousand languages, as part of the New Testament. Prior to this period, literary documents were laboriously copied manually.

During an analysis of the early Gospel documents, manuscripts handwritten on papyrus (popular in the first ten or so centuries AD) and parchment (or vellum, which is finer parchment, popular after the first couple of centuries AD), and made into scrolls or books (codices), in the first 15 centuries AD, leading up to the invention of printing, are encountered. The Greek text used in these manuscripts have either capital letters ('Uncials' or Uncial manuscripts; popular in the first millennia or so AD) or small letters in running hand writings ('Minuscules' or Minuscule manuscripts; popular after the ninth century or so AD). All papyrus manuscripts are categorised as just 'Papyrus' manuscripts without any sub classification based on the text, whereas the Greek parchment (including vellum) scrolls and codices are classified based on the writing as 'Uncials' and 'Minuscules'.

---

[1] Main source material: 'The Text of the New Testament - Its Transmission, Corruption and Restoration', Third, Enlarged Edition by Bruce M. Metzger, Oxford University Press

Documentary Evidence in Greek

There are more than 81 Greek New Testament Papyri and 266 Greek Uncials and 2754 Greek Minuscules which have been catalogued. Among these manuscripts about 50 have entire New Testaments (Codex Sinaiticus being the only Uncial in this 50) and a great majority have the 4 Gospels. Some prominent Uncial manuscripts of the Gospels from the first 5 centuries are given in Table 1.

Table 1 - Uncial Manuscripts of the Gospels (First 5 Centuries)

Ident ifier	Name	Time	Gospels Present
א	Codex Sinaiticus (Refer to Figure 1), British Library, London, UK	4th century	All 4 Gospels
A	Codex Alexandrinus (Refer to Figure 2), British Library, London, UK	5th century	Gospels apart from Matt 1:1-25:6 John 6:50-8:52
B	Codex Vaticanus, Vatican Library, Vatican City	Middle 4th century	Gospels apart from a few verses
C	Codex Ephraemi (Palimpsest[2]), Bibliothèque Nationale de France, Paris, France	5th century	Portions of all 4 Gospels

[2] Palimpsest is a manuscript or piece of writing material on which later writing has been superimposed on effaced earlier writing.

Identifier	Name	Time	Gospels Present
D	Codex Bezae, Cambridge University Library, Cambridge, UK	$5^{th}/6^{th}$ century	Most of 4 Gospels
T	Codex Borgianus, Vatican Library, Vatican City	5th century	179 verses of Luke 22-23 and John 6-8
W / 032	Codex Washingtonensis, Freer Gallery of Art, Washington DC, US	Late 4th/Early 5th century	All 4 Gospels
Z	Codex Dublinensis (Palimpsest), Trinity College Library, Dublin, Ireland	5th/6th century	295 verses of Matthew
0171	Uncial 0171, Laurentian Library, Florence and Berlin State Museum, Berlin, Germany	4th century	Matt 10:17-10:23; Matt 10:25-10:32; Luke 22:44-22:50; Luke 22:52-22:56; Luke 22:61; Luke 22:63-22:64

Although manuscripts such as ℵ, B give us a clear picture of the complete content of the Gospels from as early as the 4th century, some of the Greek Papyri fragments that we have from the couple of centuries before that will tremendously help in gaining confidence in the 1st/2nd century content of the Gospels. Bruce M. Metzger's remark - 'Just as Robinson Crusoe, seeing but a single footprint in the sand, concluded that another human being, with two feet, was present on the island with him, so P^{52} proves the existence and use of the Fourth Gospel during the first half of the second century in a provincial town along the Nile, far removed from its traditional place of composition (Ephesus in Asia Minor)' - about one of the manuscripts (P^{52}) of the Gospel of John captures the mood about the confidence of 1st century origin of the Gospels quite vividly.

Tables 2, 3, 4 and 5 give the lists of the earliest available Papyrus fragments for the Gospels Matthew, Mark, Luke and John.

Table 2 - Papyrus Fragments for Matthew (First 3 Centuries)

Identifier	Name	Time	Verses (Matthew)
P^{104}	P. Oxy. 4404, Sackler Library, Oxford, UK (Refer to Figure 3)	AD 150	21:34-21:37; 21:43-21:45
P^{64} = P^{67}	Gr. 18, Magdalen College, Oxford UK	AD 200	3; 5; 26

Identifier	Name	Time	Verses (Matthew)
P^{77}	P. Oxy. 2683 and 4405, Sackler Library, Oxford, UK	AD 200	23
P^{103}	P. Oxy. 4403, Sackler Library, Oxford, UK	AD 200	13:55-13:56; 14:3-14:5
P^{1}	P. Oxy. 2; E 2746, University of Pennsylvania, US	AD 250	1
P^{45}	BP I, Chester Beatty Library, Dublin, Ireland	AD 250	20-21; 25-26
P^{53}	Inv. 6652, University of Michigan, US	AD 250	26
P^{70}	P. Oxy. 2384, Ashmolean Museum, Oxford, UK	AD 250	2-3; 11; 12; 24
P^{101}	P. Oxy. 4401, Sackler Library, Oxford, UK	AD 250	3-4
P^{37}	P. Mich. 137; Inv. 1570, University of Michigan, US	AD 300	26
P^{102}	P. Oxy. 4402, Sackler Library, Oxford, UK	AD 300	13-14
P^{110}	P. Oxy. 4494, Sackler Library, Oxford, UK	AD 300	10:13-10:15; 25-27

Table 3 - Papyrus Fragments for Mark (First 3 Centuries)

Identifier	Name	Time	Verses (Mark)
P^{45}	BP I (Refer to Figure 4), Chester Beatty Library, Dublin, Ireland	AD 250	4-9; 11-12

Table 4 - Papyrus Fragments for Luke (First 3 Centuries)

Identifier	Name	Time	Verses (Luke)
P^{75}	P. Bodmer XIV (Refer to Figure 5), XV, Vatican Apostolic Library, Vatican City	AD 175-225	3:18-24:53
P^{4}	Suppl. Gr. 1120, National Library of France, Paris, France	AD 175-250	1-6
P^{45}	BP I, Chester Beatty Library, Dublin, Ireland	AD 250	6-7; 9-14
P^{69}	P. Oxy. 2383, Sackler Library, Oxford, UK	AD 250	22
P^{111}	P. Oxy. 4495, Sackler Library, Oxford, UK	AD 250	17
P^{7}	Petrov 553, Vernadsky National Library of Ukraine, Kiev, Ukraine	AD 300	4

Table 5 - Papyrus Fragments for John (First 3 Centuries)

Identifier	Name	Time	Verses (John)
P^{52}	Gr. P. 457 (Refer to Figure 6), John Rylands University Library, Manchester, UK	AD 125	18:31-33; 18:37-38
P^{90}	P. Oxy. 3523; 65 6 B. 32/M (3-5)a, Sackler Library, Oxford, UK	AD 150	18:36-19:1; 19:1-7
P^{75}	P. Bodmer XIV, XV, Vatican Apostolic Library, Vatican City	AD 175-225	1-15
P^{66}	P. Bodmer II, Bodmer library, Cologny, Geneva, Switzerland	AD 200	Near complete
P^{5}	P. Oxy. 208. 1781; Inv. 782. 2484, British Library, London, UK	AD 250	1; 16; 20
P^{22}	P. Oxy. 1228; MS 2-X.I, Glasgow University Library, Glasgow, UK	AD 250	15-16
P^{28}	P. Oxy. 1596; Pap. 2, Collection of Gifford Combs, Los Angeles	AD 250	6

Identifier	**Name**	**Time**	**Verses (John)**
P^{39}	P. Oxy. 1780; Inv. 8864, Green Collection, Oklahoma City, US	AD 250	8
P^{45}	BP I, Chester Beatty Library, Dublin, Ireland	AD 250	4-5; 10-11
P^{80}	Inv. 83, Fundación Sant Lluc Evangelista, Barcelo-	Ad 250	3
P^{95}	PL II/31, Laurentian Library, Florence, Italy	AD 250	5
P^{106}	P. Oxy. 4445, Sackler Library, Oxford, UK	AD 250	1
P^{107}	P. Oxy. 4446, Sackler Library, Oxford, UK	AD 250	17
P^{108}	P. Oxy. 4447, Sackler Library, Oxford, UK	AD 250	17/18
P^{109}	P. Oxy. 4448, Sackler Library, Oxford, UK	AD 250	21
P^{119}	P. Oxy. 4803, Sackler Library, Oxford, UK	AD 250	1
P^{121}	P. Oxy. 4803, Sackler Library, Oxford, UK	AD 250	19

Apart from the Greek Papyrus, Uncials and Minuscules, there are also about 2135 Greek Uncial and Minuscule lectionaries[3] which have entire or portions of New Testaments catalogued (many of which have the Gospels).

Documentary Evidence in Other Languages

Apart from the Greek manuscripts (of the Gospels and the rest of New Testaments), there is also rich manuscript evidences (more than 9,000) for the Gospels and the New Testament in a wide variety of other languages - Syriac, Latin, Coptic, Gothic, Armenian, Georgian, Ethiopic, Old Slavonic, Persian, Arabic, Nubian/Sogdian and Anglo-Saxon, dating back to, as early 4th century, some showing text form belonging to as early as 2nd century.

Syriac

There are 2 manuscripts of the Gospels (albeit with large lacunae), Syr^{c} (5th century) and Syr^{s} (4th century) both showing text forms from 2nd or beginning of 3rd century. There are about 350 manuscripts of Peshittas (5th century) - Syr^{s} in Syriac Vulgate. There are also a few other manuscripts, Philoxenian - Syr^{ph} and/or Harclean - Syr^{h} (6th/7th century) and also manuscripts in Palestinian Syriac.

---

[3] A lectionary is a book or listing that contains a collection of scripture readings appointed for Christian or Judaic worship on a given day or occasion.

Latin

There are 32 mutilated manuscripts of the Gospels in Old Latin, apart from other manuscripts for portions of the rest of the New Testament. Codex Palatinus (All Gospels; 5th century) and Codex Bobbiensis (Half of Matthew and Mark; AD 400) are some African Old Latin Gospel manuscripts and Codex Vercellensis (Before AD 370/371), Codex Vero-inensis (All Gospels; 5th century), Codex Bezae (5th/6th century) are some early European Old Latin manuscripts. There are also more than 8000 manuscripts for the Latin Vulgate version of the Bible translated by Jerome in the 4th century. Codex Sangallensis (close of 5th century), Codex Fuldensis (AD 541-546; Refer to Figure 7), Codex Mediolanensis (early 6th century) and Codex Harleianus (6th/7th century) are some early manuscripts of the Latin Vulgate Bible.

Coptic

There are also a few manuscripts of Coptic versions including in Sahidic (3rd century translations) such as Sahidic Tetraevangelium - Morgan MS. 569 (8th/9th century), Bohairic, Fayyumic (early 4th century), Sub-Achminic (AD 350-375).

Gothic

There are about half a dozen Gothic extant manuscripts (one of them nearly complete New Testament; 5th/6th century) of the 4th century translation of the Bible from Greek to Gothic by Ulfilas, an Apostle to the Goths.

Armenian

There are about 1244 manuscripts of all or part of New Testament catalogued with several hundred more estimated to be in the libraries of former USSR nations. The earliest of Armenian versions is estimated to have been revised prior to the 8th century.

Georgian

Adysh (AD 897), Opiza (AD 913) and Tbet' (AD 995) are manuscripts of Georgian translations of the New Testament. The Georgian translation is opined to have happened in the 4th century.

Ethiopic

There are a few Ethiopic manuscripts (13th century or later) of translations estimated to have been made in the 4th century (or 6th/7th century as per some).

Old Slavonic

There are manuscripts of the 9th century translations of SS. Cyril and Methodius (Apostles to Slavs).

Other

There are some Anglo-Saxon versions (7th-13th century) apart from some later manuscripts from Persian, Nubian and Sogdian.

Other Literature From Antiquity

New Testament, and especially the Gospels, are the best attested literature from antiquity (Refer to Table 6 for a comparison of the Gospels with other literature from antiquity). Commenting about this, Bruce M. Metzger says, "in evaluating the significance of these statistics of the amount of Greek evidence for the New Testament, one should consider, by way of contrast, the number of manuscripts which preserve the texts of the ancient classics. Homer's Iliad, for example, the 'bible' of the ancient Greeks, is preserved in 457 papyri, 2 uncial manuscripts and 188 minuscule manuscripts ... The works of several ancient authors are preserved to us by the thinnest possible thread of transmission ... In contrast with these figures, the textual critic of the New Testament is embarrassed by the wealth of material."

Table 6 - Comparison of Manuscript Evidence for Ancient Works[4]

Author	Date Written	Earliest Copy	Approximate Time Span between original & copy	Number of Copies	Accuracy of Copies
Lucretius	died 55 or 53 B.C.		1100 yrs	2	--
Pliny	A.D. 61-113	A.D. 850	750 yrs	7	--

[4] 'Manuscript evidence for superior New Testament reliability', Matt Slick, carm.org, 12/10/2008

Author	Date Written	Earliest Copy	Approximate Time Span between original & copy	Number of Copies	Accuracy of Copies
Plato	427-347 B.C.	A.D. 900	1200 yrs	7	--
Demosthenes	4th Cent. B.C.	A.D. 1100	800 yrs	8	--
Herodotus	480-425 B.C.	A.D. 900	1300 yrs	8	--
Suetonius	A.D. 75-160	A.D. 950	800 yrs	8	--
Thucydides	460-400 B.C.	A.D. 900	1300 yrs	8	--
Euripides	480-406 B.C.	A.D. 1100	1300 yrs	9	--
Aristophanes	450-385 B.C.	A.D. 900	1200	10	--
Caesar	100-44 B.C.	A.D. 900	1000	10	--

Author	Date Written	Earliest Copy	Approximate Time Span between original & copy	Number of Copies	Accuracy of Copies
Livy	59 BC-AD 17	--	?	20	--
Tacitus	circa A.D. 100	A.D. 1100	1000 yrs	20	--
Aristotle	384-322 B.C.	A.D. 1100	1400	49	--
Sophocle s	496-406 B.C.	A.D. 1000	1400 yrs	193	--
Homer (Iliad)	900 B.C.	400 B.C.	500 yrs	647	95%
New Testament	1stCent. A.D. (A.D. 50-100)	2nd1Cent. A.D. (c. A.D. 130 f.)	less than 100 years	5600	99.5%

Textual Criticism

To establish that the Gospels we have in use today are close enough to Jesus, it is not alone enough to find that we have richness in terms of number of manuscripts from antiquity. We also need to establish if we can have a high level of confidence in the text that we have, to be the actual text which was written in the original autographs, based on the available manuscripts from antiquity. After all, unlike in modern printing, where machines churn out quite faithfully (within certain parameters), copy after copy exactly (or near exactly) the same as the manuscript template, the method of copying documents in antiquity is manual and error strewn.

Textual criticism is a branch of textual scholarship, philology, and literary criticism that is concerned with the identification of textual variants in either manuscripts or printed books with an aim to reconstruct an unavailable original text as closely as possible.

Greg Koukl quotes[5] Daniel Wallace, 'that although there are about 300,000 individual variations of the text of the New Testament (from available manuscripts), this number is very misleading. Most of the differences are completely inconsequential - spelling errors, inverted phrases and the like. A side by side comparison between the two main text families (the Majority Text[6] and the modern critical text) shows agreement a full 98% of the time.'

---

[5] Wallace, Daniel, "The Majority Text and the Original Text: Are They Identical?," Bibliotheca Sacra, April-June, 1991, 157-8, as quoted by Greg Koukl in 'Is the New Testament Text Reliable?', str.org, 02/04/2013

[6] A specific family of New Testament text

Greg Koukl subsequently quotes[7] Geisler and Nix, 'Of the remaining differences, virtually all yield to vigorous textual criticism. This means that our New Testament is 99.5% textually pure. In the entire text of 20,000 lines, only 40 lines are in doubt (about 400 words), and none affects any significant doctrine.'

In other words, based on the corpus of manuscripts that are available to us, going back very early in the history of the Gospels and the rest of the New Testament, despite variations in the manuscripts, in applying rigorous principles of textual criticism, we are able to confidently get to 99.5% of the text of the New Testament, as written in the original autographs, by writers who were contemporaries to Jesus.

[7] Geisler, Norman L., Nix, William E., A General Introduction to the Bible (Chicago: Moody Press, 1986), as quoted by Greg Koukl in 'Is the New Testament Text Reliable?', str.org, 02/04/2013

4. Gospels - Are They Reliable Documents of History?

So far, we have been able to establish that the Gospels that we have today (i.e. the text) were indeed close enough to Jesus, whose life they are trying to portray. We also know that the Gospels were widely available (through the great wealth of the manuscripts in both the original Greek and other languages), and therefore the storyline of the Gospels was widely available for examination (either because of the circulation of the Gospels or more fundamentally because of underlying historical events and people, if the events and people were indeed historical). Moreover, the wide availability of the Gospels also means that either the text of the Gospels or the underlying historical events or people (if the events and people were indeed historical) or both were available for criticism or examination by a diverse set of people, hopefully satisfying varying expectations of qualifications needed to perform the criticism or examination. Through carefully examining recorded responses of varied and qualified people, to the storyline of the Gospels (either through reading the Gospels or through being exposed to the historical events and people portrayed in the Gospels, if at all these were historical), we may be able to come to reasonably sound judgments on the reliability of the Gospels as historical documents.

According to the Authors

At this stage, it is fair to give the writers of the Gospels a chance to introduce their own works. In our current stage of evaluation, it is not important to verify who wrote the Gospels, as much as it is important to verify the reliability of what was written in the Gospels. Nevertheless, the traditional identities of the writers of the Gospels have been pointed out right away, if not for anything else, at least for referencing passages from the Gospels easily.

The writer of the first Gospel, traditionally identified as Matthew ('Matt' in references), a tax-collector turned Apostle (official-emissary) of Jesus begins his Gospel thus - 'The book of the genealogy of Jesus Christ, the Son of David, the Son of Abraham' [Matt 1:1]. He then carries ahead through his narration with expressions such as 'Now after Jesus was born in Bethlehem of Judea in the days of Herod the king' [Matt 2:1], 'In those days John the Baptist came preaching' [Matt 3:1] and 'they led him away and delivered Him to Pontius Pilate the governor' [Matt 27:2]. He brings in names of many specific people and people groups and describes events and places, not at any point giving any indication that he was trying to record anything other than what he perceived to be based on true historical people, events and places.

The writer of the second Gospel, is traditionally identified as John Mark ('Mark' in references), a relative of an early Church leader, namely Barnabas, and someone in close proximity to different Apostles of Jesus at different times, namely Paul (formerly Saul) and later Simon Peter. In his Gospel, similar to Matthew, he refers to specific people and people groups, describes events and places, all the time giving an impression that he was recording what he perceived to be accounts of true historical people, events and places.

The writer of the third Gospel, is traditionally identified as Luke ('Luke' in references), a Physician by profession and a companion of Paul, an Apostle of Jesus. He begins his Gospel saying, 'Inasmuch as many have taken in hand to set in order a narrative of those things which have been fulfilled among us, just as those who from the beginning were eyewitnesses and ministers of the word delivered them to us, it seemed good to me also, having had perfect understanding of all things from the very first, to write to you an an orderly account, most excellent Theophilus' [Luke 1:1-1:3]. His intent in writing his Gospel is quite clear at the outset, to write an 'orderly account' having had 'perfect understanding' of all things which have been 'fulfilled' in his neighbourhood.

The fourth Gospel, which is traditionally attributed to John ('John' in references), an Apostle of Jesus, seems to have been written by someone who was uniquely qualified to be called 'the disciple whom Jesus loved' [John 21:20; John 21:24] and to have been jointly testified by multiple people [John 21:24] ('we know that his testimony is true'). He also, like the other Gospel-writers refers to specific people and people groups, describes events and places, all the time giving an impression that he was recording what he perceived to be accounts of true historical people, events and places.

Admittedly, unlike a writer of a typical 21st century historical work, the Gospel writers had additional agenda, on top of producing a historical record of the life of Jesus, and that was to convince people of certain aspects of the identity of Jesus which, according to the writers, uniquely qualified him to be identified as God. In other words, the Gospels, on top of being documents of history also go on to be documents of theology. It is best to emphasize again, that in this section, our concern would be broadly to establish the reliability of the Gospels as documents of history or in other words to establish the veracity of the 'historical aspects' and not so much the 'theological aspects' (which we would address in a later stage, if the Gospels qualify to even get to that stage after coming clean as reliable documents of history).

Evaluation of Historical Context Used in the Gospels

'It is better to keep your mouth shut and appear stupid than open it and remove all doubt' says an old adage. This is very applicable for a work of history also. Even though a work has to have 'some history' recorded for it to be qualified to be called 'a work of history', the moment it records a wide variety of information it becomes susceptible to get at least some of the recordings inaccurate or not as accurate as it would like to get it. This would have a tremendous detriment in its reliability as a historical account (We can imagine people asking questions such as 'if it is wrong about this fact A, how are we to trust in its other claims?'). Despite this threat, the Gospels record a wide variety of detail about 1st century life. This is a great boon in our current quest of establishing whether the Gospels are reliable documents of history, because we could try and see if these details are reasonably accurate.

People

A number of people have been referred to in the Gospels. A considerable number of them have been verified through extra Biblical sources. John the Baptist [Matt 3:1; Mark 1:4; Luke 3:2; John 1:6] has been verified through writings of Josephus, a Jewish historian (Antiquities of the Jews - Book 18, 5.2). The family of King Herod [Matt 2:1; Luke 1:5], including his sons, Herod Archelaus [Matt 2:22], Herod Antipas - Tetrarch of Galilee [Matt 14:1; Mark 6:14; Luke 3:1] and Philip - Tetrarch of Iturea and the region of Trachonitis (brother of Herod Antipas) [Mark 6:17; Luke 3:1] have been verified through Herodian coinage (Refer to Figures 8-11). Lysanias - Tetrarch of Abilene [Luke 3:1] is believed to have been referred to, in a temple inscription found at Abila.

Quirinius - Governor of Syria [Luke 2:2] is referred to, in the works of Josephus (Antiquities of the Jews - Book 18, 1.1). Augustus Caesar [Luke 2:1] and Tiberius Caesar [Luke 3:1] are Roman emperors widely attested in history (Refer to Figures 12 and 13). Pontius Pilate [Matt 27:2; Mark 15:1; Luke 3:1; John 18:29] has been verified through the Pilate Stone inscription (Refer to Figure 14). Annas [Luke 3:2; John 18:13] and Caiaphas [Matt 26:3; Luke 3:2; John 11:49] have been verified through the works of Josephus (Antiquities of the Jews - Book 20, 9.1 and Book 18, 2.2 respectively).

Politics

The Gospel writers show reasonable sensitivity to subtle differences in power in the region, as understood through an extensive study of extra Biblical artefacts. Herod the Great is rightly said to have been 'King' [Matt 2:1; Luke 1:5] over the Kingdom of Judea [Matt 2:22; Luke 1:5] whereas his sons Herod Archelaus, Herod Antipas and Philip are said to have been Tetrarchs [Matt 14:1; Luke 3:1] over smaller regions called Judea [Matt 2:22; Luke 3:1], Galilee [Luke 3:1] and Iturea and Trachonitis [Luke 3:1] respectively. It is Mark alone who refers to Herod Antipas, Tetrarch of Galilee, as a 'King' [Mark 6:14] but the context of his writing indicates that his rulership was over Galilee (a reduced region) and not the Kingdom of Judea (a larger region) as his father. Pilate and Quirinius are rightly said to have been Governors [Matt 27:2; Luke 3:1; Luke 2:2] as they were really governing what were Roman provinces. Pilate's official title was Prefect as per Pilate Stone inscription. Lysanias is also rightly called as a Tetrarch [Luke 3:1] and this is believed to have been verified through a temple inscription found at Abila.

The tensions that existed between the people of the occupied region (Jews especially) and the occupying powers were also clearly understood and captured. These come out through communications about Caesar [Luke 23:2; John 19:12], expressions such as 'expedient that one man should die' [John 11:50; John 18:14], 'if we let Him alone like this, everyone will believe in Him, and the Romans will come and take away both our place and nation' [John 11:48] and record of a rebellion by Barabbas [Matt 27:16; Mark 15:7; Luke 23:18; John 18:40]. Even tensions which might escape common knowledge have been noted and recorded - enmity between Pilate and Herod [Luke 23:12].

Events

The Gospels record Caesar Augustus ordering a census [Luke 2:1-2:3] that first took place when Quirinius was governor of Syria [Luke 2:2]. Josephus records (Antiquities of the Jews - Book 18, 1.1) how Quirinius has conducted censuses like this.

Events in the accounts of the Gospels - death of Herod [Matt 2:15, 2:19], Jesus' conception in the sixth month of John the Baptist's conception [Luke 1:26], John's ministry commencing on the fifteenth year of reign of Tiberius Caesar (Pontius Pilate being governor of Judea, Herod being tetrarch of Galilee, his brother Philip tetrarch of Iturea and the region of Trachonitis, and Lysanias tetrarch of Abilene, while Annas and Caiaphas were high priests) [Luke 3:1] - are reasonably synchronous with extra Biblical references to these events.

There are also other notable events mentioned - Pilate mingling blood of Galileans with their sacrifice [Luke 13:1] and eighteen killed by the falling of the tower in Siloam [Luke 13:4] - which are open to being scrutinized.

Languages

The languages in use in the region are accurately captured by the record of the languages of inscription on the cross - Hebrew, Greek, and Latin [Matt 27:35-27:44; Mark 15:24-15:32; Luke 23:33-23:43; John 19:18-19:27]. The only other language which would have been in use in the region as per our modern understanding is also recorded to have been in use - Aramaic [Matt 27:46; Mark 15:34].

Finance

Details about money recorded in the Gospels seem reasonable based on our understanding of the region and time. Some of the currencies recorded are - stater [Matt 17:27] (Refer to Figure 15), two denarii [Luke 10:35] (Refer to Figure 16), denarius [Matt 20:2; Mark 12:15; Luke 20:24], assarion [Luke 12:6] (Refer to Figure 17), lepton [Luke 12:59], two Lepta, which make a quadrans [Mark 12:42; Luke 21:2] (Refer to Figure 18), drachma [Luke 15:8] (Refer to Figure 19) and minas [Luke 19:11-19:27].

The record about temple tax [Matt 17:24] seems to show an awareness of the Jewish temple tax [Exodus 30:13]. The requirement of transactions in the Jerusalem Temple to be made in Jewish or Tyrian money and not in the common Greek or Roman currency makes the record about Temple money exchange [Matt 21:12; Mark 11:15; John 2:14] reasonable. Also, the record of tax to be paid to Caesar [Matt 22:17; Mark 12:14; Luke 20:22] is consistent with extra Biblical records.

Religion

Record of some details of the Jerusalem Temple duties - 'while he was serving as priest before God in the order of his division (Abijah), according to the custom of his priesthood' [Luke 1:5; Luke 1:8] and 'the days of his service were completed' [Luke 1:23] is consistent with the Jewish tradition [1 Chronicles 24:3-24:18]. Depiction of synagogues [Matt 10:17; Mark 13:9; Luke 12:11; John 16:2] as the prominent places of gathering, next only in prominence to the Temple, is consistent with the Jewish tradition. Records of some of the behavioural patterns - the raising of some Sabbath related issues [Matt 12:2; Mark 2:23; Luke 6:1; John 5:10], not wanting to enter into the Praetorium on a preparation day [John 18:18], not wanting a corpse to be on the cross on the Sabbath [John 19:31], manner of purification of the Jews [John 2:6], custom of the feast [Luke 2:42], Jews gathering in Jerusalem for the passover and that too a few days early to purify themselves [John 11:55], having waterpots to be used in purification [John 2:6], corban [Mark 7:11], wearing phylacteries [Matt 23:5], burying the dead [Matt 8:21; Luke 9:59; John 19:40], burying in a nearby place in order to be prepare for the Sabbath [John 19:42] are all reasonable in the Jewish tradition.

Record of Annas wielding much power despite Caiaphas being the actual High Priest [Luke 3:2; John 18:24] is consistent with Josephus' record that Annas was 'the most fortunate man' (Antiquities of the Jews - Book 20, 9.1).

Treatment of Samaritans [Luke 10:33; John 4:9] is consistent with the Jewish records.

Expectation of a promised Messiah, Elijah and the Prophet [Mark 6:14-6:15; Luke 9:8; John 1:20-1:23][Matt 11:7-11:11; Matt 11:14; Luke 7:24-7:28] [Matt 16:14; Mark 8:28; Luke 9:19] [Matt 17:10-17:13; Mark 9:11-9:13] expressed in different forms including as expecting salvation by Zacharias [Luke 1:68-1:79] and Simeon [Luke 2:29-2:32] seems to be reasonable given the expectations set by Jewish scriptures [Malachi 3-4].

Society

Portrayals of different groups in the society - Samaritans [Luke 10:33; John 4:9], Pharisees [Matt 3:7; Mark 2:16; Luke 5:17; John 1:24], Sadducees [Matt 3:7; Mark 12:18; Luke 20:27], Scribes [Matt 2:4; Mark 2:16; Luke 5:21; John 8:3], Lawyers [Matt 22:35; Luke 7:30], Elders [Matt 16:21; Mark 8:31; Luke 20:1], Chief Priests [Matt 2:4; Mark 11:18; Luke 19:47; John 7:32], High Priest [Matt 26:3; Mark 14:53; Luke 22:54; John 11:49], Council (Sanhedrin) [Matt 26:59; Mark 14:55; Luke 22:66; John 11:47], Levites [Luke 10:32; John 1:19], Tax Collectors and sinners [Matt 9:10; Mark 2:15; Luke 5:30] - are consistent with the portrayals of these groups in extra-Biblical sources.

Geography

Fig tree [Matt 21:19; Mark 11:13; Luke 13:6; John 1:48], mustard seed [Matt 13:31; Mark 4:31; Luke 13:19] and grapes [Matt 20:1; Mark 12:1; Luke 13:6] are part of the flora of the region.

Some of the geographical aspects like - Nazareth built on a hill [Luke 4:29], changing water levels in river Jordan [John 3:23], Brook Kidron [John 18:1], Mount Olivet [Luke 19:29], Sea of Tiberias [John 6:1], Garden beyond brook Kidron [John 18:1] are all reasonable features in the region.

Places

Places matching descriptions of Pool of Bethesda [John 5:2] and Siloam pool [John 9:7] have been excavated in modern times.

Time

Expressions of time such as 'about the tenth hour' [John 1:39], 'about the sixth hour' [John 4:6], 'at the seventh hour and in the same hour' [John 4:52-4:53], 'fourth watch' [Mark 6:48] and 'second watch' [Luke 12:38] seem to be reasonable for a 1st century Jewish account.

Crux of the Gospels

Having established that the context used in the Gospels for the narration of the life of Jesus is reasonably accurate, our next task would be to evaluate the actual storyline of the life of Jesus. Afterall, even a fictional story could be set in a reasonably accurate historical context. But if the core storyline of Jesus' life is justified, through reasonable means, to be historically reliable, then we would have a historical person in Jesus relating to historical people in historical events in a historical setting i.e. a true work of history out and out. That sounds terrific, but now the challenge is in establishing exactly the crucial elements that reasonably comprehensively cover the crux of the story line. Without doubt, the elements would include a uniquely identifiable Jesus, extravagant claims, a set of followers or disciples, miracles, teachings distinct from traditional Judaism, conflict with religious authorities, accusation, condemnation, crucifixion, resurrection, worship of Jesus by his disciples and the spreading of news about him. Now it is reasonable to expect even non-Christian sources to validate some elements like extravagant claims, a set of followers or disciples etc, as these elements might have been played out in the eyes of non-disciples also. However, what are we to do with some elements, which we may find in the Gospels narration, that may have been played out in the eyes of only disciples. Most notable of this would be the actual resurrection - where only disciples saw the resurrected Jesus. Nice catch. Does that mean, once we verify other elements to be historically reliable, not expecting to see non-disciple first hand account of the resurrection, we just look like the cat that swallowed the canary, in pretending we have verified the historical reliability of all the elements of the crux? Not really - and this may come as a relief to some of us. In verifying the historical reliability of the crux of the Gospels, we could afford to make some 'approximations', and delay the verification of the 'actuals' as opposed to the 'approximations', to when we get a chance to grill the disciples about their testimonies. For instance, instead of expecting a non-disciple first hand account of the 'resurrection' itself, we could comfortably use a non-disciple first hand account of "disciples' belief in Jesus' resurrection" for now. After this approximation, we could try and verify the existence of the belief in Jesus' resurrection to establish that the crux of the Gospels is historically reliable. This is exactly the replacement we would make in our crux, in this section. In later sections, we would then try and see if the disciples' belief in the resurrection of Jesus is rational and evidential.

Element 1: Particular Jesus

The name 'Jesus' (in its Hebrew form) was a very popular Jewish name in history, especially in the 1st century. The name 'James' (a half-brother of Jesus) was also another very popular Jewish name. However, the Jesus of the Gospels, who had a half brother called James could be uniquely identified by the title that was attributed to him in the Gospels, namely - Messiah or Christ.

This element of the crux can be therefore stated as - the Particular Jesus of the Gospels was a Jesus [Matt 1:21; Mark 1:9; Luke 1:31; John 1:29] who was given the title, Christ [Matt 1:1; Mark 1:1; Luke 9:20; John 1:17], who had a half brother called James [Matt 13:55; Mark 6:3] and lived in the 1st century [Matt 2:15; Matt 2:19; Luke 1:26; Luke 3:1].

Element 2: Disciples

The particular Jesus of the Gospels had picked up multiple disciples [Matt 10:1; Mark 3:13] over the course of his public life. Some of these disciples were also called Apostles (official-emissaries) [Matt 10:1; Mark 3:13; Luke 6:13] of Jesus.

Element 3: Extravagant Claims

The particular Jesus of the Gospels, even by Jewish standards of bold claims made by various prophets, had many bold, public claims attributed to himself. For instance, he was claimed to be Son of God [Matt 3:16-3:17; Mark 1:10-1:11; Luke 1:35; Luke 3:22; John 1:32-1:34], One greater than the Temple [Matt 12:6], Lord of the Sabbath [Matt 12:8; Mark 2:28; Luke 6:5], someone who was one with the Jewish God [John 10:30], teacher [Matt 19:16; Mark 10:17; Luke 18:18; John 20:16], prophet [Matt 13:57; Mark 6:4; John 4:44] and king [Matt 27:11; Mark 15:2; Luke 23:3; John 18:36].

Element 4: New Teaching

Jesus' teachings (called as new wine by Jesus himself) couldn't be contained within traditional Judaism [Matt 9:17; Mark 1:27; Luke 5:37].

Element 5: Miracles

Jesus performed many miracles [Matt 8:14-8:17; Mark 1:29-1:34; Luke 4:38-4:41; John 5:1-5:47].

Element 6: Dying Messiah - An Alien Idea

Even towards the end of Jesus' time in public ministry, the Jews hadn't expected that their true Messiah (Christ) would die [John 12:34].

Element 7: Jewish Leadership Offended

Jewish leadership during Jesus' time were offended overall by Jesus. They attributed his miracles to demons [Matt 12:24; Mark 3:22; Luke 11:15] and questioned his authority [Matt 21:23; Mark 11:28; Luke 20:2].

Element 8: Jewish Plan to Destroy Jesus

Jewish leadership had planned to destroy Jesus much ahead of the actual crucifixion. The Pharisees and the Herodians had planned to destroy him perhaps more than a year before the actual crucifixion [Matt 12:14; Mark 3:6; Luke 6:11], but all of Jewish leadership agreed to destroy him perhaps a few weeks before the actual crucifixion [John 11:45-11:54].

Element 9: Jewish Accusation

Jewish leadership during Jesus' time were instrumental in getting Jesus condemned to capital punishment [Matt 27:12; Mark 15:14; Luke 23:21; John 19:6].

Element 10: Roman Condemnation

Jesus was condemned to be crucified by Roman prefect Pontius Pilate [Matt 27:24; Mark 15:15; Luke 23:24; John 19:16]

Element 11: Crucifixion

Jesus was executed by crucifixion [Matt 20:19; Mark 15:15; Luke 23:21; Luke 23:24; John 19:16]

Element 12: Nature's Response to Crucifixion

There was darkness for 3 hours at midday during Jesus' crucifixion [Matt 27:45; Mark 15:33; Luke 23:44] and the earth quaked [Matt 27:51]

Element 13: Disciples' Belief in Jesus' Resurrection

Jesus' disciples believed that Jesus had risen up after he was dead and buried [Matt 28:17; Mark 16:14; Luke 24:36-24:43; John 20:19-20:25]. This was evident in Peter's and others' preaching [Acts[8] 2:24].

Element 14: Disciples Worship Jesus

Jesus was considered to be God, by his disciples and was worshipped as such [Matt 28:9; Matt 28:17; Luke 24:52]

Element 15: Persecution of the Early Church in Jerusalem

Early Church faced much persecution right in Jerusalem for their beliefs [Acts 5:18] and were forbidden from spreading news about Jesus [Acts 4:18]. Some of them even became martyrs in Jerusalem [Acts 7:57-7:60].

[8] The book of Acts is a sequel to the Gospel of Luke written by the same Luke who wrote the Gospel of Luke. Refer to Appendix 1 for documentary evidence for this book.

Element 16: Growth of the Early Church in Jerusalem

Many new disciples were added to the Church after the purported resurrection of Jesus [Acts 2:41; Acts 5:14], right in Jerusalem.

Evaluation of the Crux of the Gospels

There are a number of Roman, Jewish and Greek sources that give us extra Biblical details about Jesus. These sources, from the point of the Christian message, can be considered to be at least unbiased even if not anti-biased, and therefore may act as good witnesses to the historical reliability of the Gospels accounts. There would be reason to rejoice, if these sources, put together, can help us verify almost all the elements of the crux of the Gospels, listed out in the previous section, from a non-disciple viewpoint.

Evidence 1: Tacitus - Annals XV.44

Gaius Cornelius Tacitus (AD 56 - AD 118) was a Roman senator, orator and ethnographer, and arguably the best[9] of Roman historians. In his last major work, titled 'Annals', written c. AD 116-117, Tacitus mentions about Christians in the context of Emperor Nero trying to use the Christians as a scapegoat for a fire that burnt part of Rome in AD 64.

'But neither human help, nor imperial munificence, nor all the modes of placating Heaven, could stifle scandal or dispel the belief that the fire had taken place by order. Therefore, to scotch the rumour, Nero substituted as culprits, and punished with the utmost refinements of cruelty, a class of men, loathed for their vices, whom the crowd styled christians. Chri-

[9] 'Did Jesus Exist? Searching for Evidence Beyond the Bible', Lawrence Mykytiuk, www.biblicalarchaeology.org, 18/11/2015

stus, the founder of the name, had undergone the death penalty in the reign of Tiberius, by sentence of the procurator Pontius Pilatus, and the pernicious superstition was checked for a moment, only to break out once more, not merely in Judaea, the home of the disease, but in the capital itself, where all things horrible or shameful in the world collect and find a vogue.'[10]

This passage gives evidence for a number of the elements of the crux of the Gospels. It records a person with the name Christ (Element 1) whose followers were called Christians (Element 2). Lawrence Mykytiuk[11] notes that Tacitus records Christians as Chrestians. Usage of the name Chrestians was a 'misunderstanding of the "crowd" (vulgus)', which Tacitus corrects by 'by stating that the founder of this name (auctor nominis eius) is Christus, not the name implicitly given by the crowd, Chrestus'. This Christ was executed in the reign of Tiberius by the procurator Pontius Pilate (Element 10). Tacitus goes on to rightly point out that the group 'Christians', had their origin in Judea, but by the time of the fire in Rome, during Nero's time, had reached Rome also. The severity communicated in the word 'break out' could very well indicate that there was forceful attempt to contain the belief of the disciples (Element 15). The expression 'break out once more, not merely in Judaea' indicates that the 'pernicious superstition' had 'broken out' at least twice in Judea, meaning there was an initial growth (Element 16) before an attempted suppression (Element 15) and a subsequent growth.

There are a few expressions that Tacitus uses in regards to the beliefs of the Christians - 'vices', 'pernicious superstition', 'disease'.

---

[10]http://penelope.uchicago.edu/Thayer/E/Roman/Texts/Tacitus/Annals/15B*.html, 03/12/2015

[11] 'Did Jesus Exist? Searching for Evidence Beyond the Bible', Lawrence Mykytiuk, www.biblicalarchaeology.org, 18/11/2015

Exactly what was the 'vice', the 'pernicious superstition' and the 'disease' in the beliefs of Christians is not clarified in the immediate context. However, it would be reasonable to think that the idea of resurrection as we know through the Gospels might have been obnoxious even in the context of the Roman religion, for a Roman priest[12] (Element 13). Christians are also said to have been 'loathed'.

Evidence 2: Josephus - Antiquities of the Jews - Book 20, 9.1

Jewish historian Josephus (AD 37-100) is noted for his two works, 'Antiquities of the Jews' and 'The Jewish War'.

In one of the references about Jesus (Antiquities of the Jews - 20.9.1), he notes, 'when, therefore, Ananus was of this disposition, he thought he had now a proper opportunity [to exercise his authority]. Festus was now dead, and Albinus was but upon the road; so he assembled the Sanhedrin of judges, and brought before them the brother of Jesus, who was called Christ, whose name was James, and some others [or, some of his companions]; and when he had formed an accusation against them as breakers of the law, he delivered them to be stoned.'[13]

In this passage, Josephus identifies the particular Jesus of the Gospels, in the context of his brother, James (Element 1).

He mentions that James and some others had been accused as 'breakers of the law' and were 'delivered ... to be stoned'. He doesn't clarify what exact law was broken. If the transgression that is being referred to here

---

[12] In AD 88, Tacitus became a member of the 'Quindecimviri Sacris Faciundis' ['The Board of Fifteen for Performing Sacrifices'] a Roman priestly organization
[13] Jewish Antiquities, translated by William Whiston, 'The New Complete Works of Josephus', Kregel Publications.

is the actual following of Jesus' teaching, then this is another evidence that the early Church was persecuted right in Jerusalem.

Evidence 3: Josephus - Antiquities of the Jews - Book 18, 3.3

In 'Antiquities of the Jews - Book 18, 3.3' Josephus notes, 'Now there was about this time Jesus, a wise man, *if it be lawful to call him a man*; for he was a doer of wonderful works, a teacher of such men as receive the truth with pleasure. He drew over to him both many of the Jews and many of the Gentiles. *He was [the] Christ.* And when Pilate, at the suggestion of the principal men among us, had condemned him to the cross, those that loved him at the first did not forsake him; *for he appeared to them alive again the third day, as the divine prophets had foretold these and ten thousand other wonderful things concerning him.* And the tribe of Christians, so named from him, are not extinct at this day.'[14]

The italicised portions are considered perhaps not to be from Josephus himself, and are likely to be changes made after him, as the 'Christian' tone in these portions are not considered Jewish enough for a Jew like Josephus who stuck to Judaism even after Jesus.

Even ignoring the italicised portions, a number of elements of the crux of the Gospels are attested by Josephus. The particular Jesus of the Gospels has been identified in his 'Jesus, a wise man … the tribe of Christians, so named from him' (Element 1). The fact that Jesus had disciples even during his lifetime is attested to by the remarks 'a teacher of such men as receive the truth with pleasure', 'He drew over to him both many of the Jews and many of the Gentiles' and 'the tribe of Christians, so

[14] Jewish Antiquities, translated by William Whiston, 'The New Complete Works of Josephus', Kregel Publications.

named from him, are not extinct at this day' (Element 2). The fact that Jesus had teachings distinct from traditional Judaism of that time is clarified through the expression 'drew over' in the 'drew over to him both many of the Jews' to form a 'tribe of Christians' (Element 4). Jesus is said to have performed 'wonderful works', most likely an expression meaning miracles (Element 5). Jesus is said to have been accused by 'principal men among us' (Element 9) and eventually condemned by Pontius Pilate (Element 10) to be crucified (Element 11).

Evidence 4: Pliny the Younger - Epistles X.96

Gaius Plinius Caecilius Secundus (AD 61–113), known as Pliny the Younger is a Roman Governor and friend of Tacitus. In his lengthy letter to Emperor Trajan (Epistles X.96) asking for guidance as to how to deal with Christians he notes[15], 'In the meanwhile, the method I have observed towards those who have been denounced to me as Christians is this: I interrogated them whether they were Christians; if they confessed it I repeated the question twice again, adding the threat of capital punishment; if they still persevered, I ordered them to be executed. For whatever the nature of their creed might be, I could at least feel no doubt that contumacy and inflexible obstinacy deserved chastisement. There were others also possessed with the same infatuation, but being citizens of Rome, I directed them to be carried thither.', 'They affirmed, however, the whole of their guilt, or their error, was, that they were in the habit of meeting on a certain fixed day before it was light, when they sang in alternate verses a hymn to Christ, as to a god, and bound themselves by a solemn oath, not to any wicked deeds, but never to commit any fraud, theft or adultery, never to falsify their word, nor deny a trust

[15] http://www.vroma.org/~hwalker/Pliny/Pliny10-096-E.html

when they should be called upon to deliver it up; after which it was their custom to separate, and then reassemble to partake of food but food of an ordinary and innocent kind.' and 'I therefore adjourned the proceedings, and betook myself at once to your counsel. For the matter seemed to me well worth referring to you, especially considering the numbers endangered. Persons of all ranks and ages, and of both sexes are, and will be, involved in the prosecution. For this contagious superstition is not confined to the cities only, but has spread through the villages and rural districts; it seems possible, however, to check and cure it.'

Pliny verifies the presence of disciples of Jesus (Christians) during his time of writing the letter (around AD 110) (Element 2). The expression 'they sang … as to a god' establishes that the Jews worshipped Jesus (Element 14). His record of the 'contumacy and inflexible obstinacy' despite the threat of capital punishment and actual execution of Christians in Bithynia (where Pliny was a Governor) makes it very likely that disciples might have been very likely persecuted in Jerusalem also, a city under another Roman Governor (Element 15). Furthermore, Pliny records that belief in Christ had 'spread' to 'all ranks and ages', 'both sexes', 'villages and rural districts' indicating the growth of the church in Bithynia.

The term 'contagious superstition' could be reasonable if Pliny was in fact referring to belief in Jesus' resurrection, as such a belief would be quite extra-ordinary in the context of even in the context of Roman religion (Element 13).

Evidence 5: Suetonius - The Lives of the Twelve Caesars - Book V, 25.4

Gaius Suetonius Tranquillus (AD 70–140), was a Roman historian. In his work 'On the lives of Caesars' he notes of an event which happened in AD 49, 'Since the Jews constantly made disturbances at the instigation of Chrestus, he expelled them from Rome.'[16]

With Jews as the context, this 'Chrestus' can be understood as 'Christ' (Element 1). However, there are some difficulties in this evaluation as Suetonius seems to indicate that it was Chrestus who was actively instigating the Jews to make disturbances.

Evidence 6: Suetonius - The Lives of the Twelve Caesars - Book VI, 16.2

Suetonius, in his record of Emperor Nero mentions, 'Punishment was inflicted on the Christians, a class of men given to a new and mischievous superstition'[17].

This is a record for the existence of Jesus' disciples (Element 2). The term 'new and mischievous superstition' could be reasonable if Suetonius was in fact referring to belief in Jesus' resurrection, as such a belief would be quite extra-ordinary in the context of even in the context of Roman religion (Element 13).

---

[16]http://penelope.uchicago.edu/Thayer/E/Roman/Texts/Suetonius/12Caesars/Claudius*.html

[17]http://penelope.uchicago.edu/Thayer/E/Roman/Texts/Suetonius/12Caesars/Nero*.html

Evidence 7: Lucian of Samosata - The Passing of Peregrinus

Lucian of Samosata (AD 115–200) was a Greek satirist who wrote *The Passing of Peregrinus*, about a former Christian who later became a famous Cynic and revolutionary and died in AD 165.

In his work, two particular passages[18] are relevant - 'It was then that he learned the wondrous lore of the Christians, by associating with their priests and scribes in Palestine. And—how else could it be?—in a trice he made them all look like children, for he was prophet, cult-leader, head of the synagogue, and everything, all by himself. He interpreted and explained some of their books and even composed many, and they revered him as a god, made use of him as a lawgiver, and set him down as a protector, next after that other, to be sure, whom they still worship, the man who was crucified in Palestine because he introduced this new cult into the world.' and 'The poor wretches have convinced themselves, first and foremost, that they are going to be immortal and live for all time, in consequence of which they despise death and even willingly give themselves into custody; most of them. Furthermore, their first lawgiver persuaded them that they are all brothers of one another after they have transgressed once, for all by denying the Greek gods and by worshipping that crucified sophist himself and living under his laws. Therefore they despise all things indiscriminately and consider them common property, receiving such doctrines traditionally without any definite evidence. So if any charlatan and trickster, able to profit by occasions, comes among them, he quickly acquires sudden wealth by imposing upon simple folk.'

[18] http://www.tertullian.org/rpearse/lucian/peregrinus.htm

These two passages vouch for a number of elements of the crux of the Gospels.

Christians here are identified as both Jews (because of the expression 'interpreted and explained some of their books', where 'their books' would be the Old Testament) and possibly gentiles (if 'denying the Greek gods' means giving up on previous worship of Greek gods). Jesus is seen to have offended (presumably the Jewish leadership) through the expression, 'he introduced this new cult into the world' (Element 7), and was crucified (Element 11). Jesus is noted also as having been worshipped (Element 14). Expressions such as 'despise death' and 'willingly give themselves into custody' communicate that there was persecution of the disciples. This persecution is most likely the one suffered by early disciples right in Judea, given the context of the passage, which is about a learning from 'priests and scribes in Palestine' (Element 15).

Expressions that Lucian uses such as 'convinced themselves, first and foremost, that they are going to be immortal', 'live for all time' and 'despise death' are perhaps the best attestations of the early Christian belief in resurrection (directly) and Jesus' resurrection (indirectly). Christians that Lucian is talking about most certainly included Jews also (as expressed through the comment, 'interpreted and explained some of their books'). Not all Jews might have believed in heaven (for instance Sadducees didn't believe in resurrection of the dead). Those who did believe in heaven, before Christ, might not have manifested their views of heaven through actions demanding comments such as 'convinced themselves, first and foremost, that they are going to be immortal', 'live for all time' and 'despise death'. These comments have an overtone related to 'defeating death', which would make much sense if the Jews that Lucian has referred to, believed in Christ's resurrection, making 'defeating death' as their primary lens with which they see heaven (Element 13).

Evidence 8: Celsus, a Platonist Philosopher

Origen, a 2nd century Christian leader, in his work 'Against Celsus', deals with accusations that Celsus, a Platonist Philosopher brings up against Jesus in the 2nd century. Referring to Celsus' accusation, Origen says 'Next he makes the charge of the savior that it was by magic that he was able to do the miracles which he appeared to have done, and foreseeing that others also, having learned the same lessons and being haughty to act with the power of God, are about to do the same thing, such persons Jesus would drive away from his own society. For he says, "He was brought up in secret and hired himself out as a workman in Egypt, and having tried his hand at certain magical powers he returned from there, and on account of those powers gave himself the title of God"'.[19]

According to Origen's quotation, Celsus notes that Jesus was identified as God (Element 3; Presumably Element 14 also) and was said to have magical powers (Element 5) which Celsus attributes to Jesus' early life in Egypt.

Evidence 9: Babylonian Talmud

The Tract Sanhedrin (Sanhedrin 43a), which is part of a 2nd century compilation of Jewish Rabbinical writings has a passage that seems to be a reference to Jesus of the Gospels, 'On the eve of the Passover Yeshu [Jesus] was hanged. For forty days before the execution took place,

[19] Origen, Against Celsus, 1.6, 38, as translated in Evans, "Jesus in Non-Christian Sources," p. 460 as reproduced in 'Did Jesus Exist? Searching for Evidence Beyond the Bible', Lawrence Mykytiuk, www.biblicalarchaeology.org, 18/11/2015

a herald went forth and cried, "He is going forth to be stoned because he has practised sorcery and enticed Israel to apostasy.'"

This passage identifies Jesus as someone who was hanged on the eve of the Passover (Element 1). He is accused to have practiced sorcery (Element 5) and is said to have enticed Israel to apostasy apparently indicating that following his teaching amounts to as much as 'apostasy' in the context of traditional Judaism as seen by some (Element 4). The fact that the Jewish leadership was offended is clarified by the fact that Jesus' practice was even paid attention to for a response (Element 7). The Jewish leaders had planned to execute Jesus well ahead (40 days) of the actual Passover crucifixion (Element 8). The Jewish leaders would have been very well open to accusing him before a Roman Governor based on their decision to stone him (Element 9). He is said to have been hanged, which seems to have been a term used in reference to crucifixion also in other parts of New Testament [Acts 5:30] (Element 11).

Evidence 10: Thallus[20]

Thallus wrote a history of the eastern Mediterranean world since the Trojan War. His original writing is lost. We however have, Julius Africanus, a renowned 3rd century historian quoting him thus: 'Thallus, in the third book of his histories, explains away the darkness as an eclipse of the sun—unreasonably as it seems to me.' Africanus' point was about Thallus misinterpreting the darkness that covered the earth during the crucifixion to be a solar eclipse (Element 12).

[20] Source: 'Darkness at the crucifixion: metaphor or real history?', Daniel Anderson, creation.com, 6/4/2007

Evidence 11: Phlegon[21]

Phlegon, a Greek historian, who wrote an extensive chronology in AD 137 wrote, "In the fourth year of the 202nd Olympiad (i.e., AD 33) there was 'the greatest eclipse of the sun' and that 'it became night in the sixth hour of the day [i.e., noon] so that stars even appeared in the heavens. There was a great earthquake in Bithynia, and many things were overturned in Nicaea."

This quotation is related to the sun darkening and the earth quaking during crucifixion (Element 12).

Evidence 12: Africanus[22]

Africanus composed a five volume 'History of the World' around AD 221. In his work, Africanus argues that the darkness on the earth during crucifixion (Element 12) can not be a result of solar eclipse, 'On the whole world there pressed a most fearful darkness; and the rocks were rent by an earthquake, and many places in Judea and other districts were thrown down. This darkness Thallus, in the third book of his *History*, calls, as appears to me without reason, an eclipse of the sun. For the Hebrews celebrate the passover on the 14th day according to the moon, and the passion of our Savior falls on the day before the passover; but an eclipse of the sun takes place only when the moon comes under the sun. And it cannot happen at any other time but in the interval between the first day of the new moon and the last of the old, that is, at their junction: how then should an eclipse be supposed to happen when the moon is almost diametrically opposite the sun? Let opinion pass however; let it carry the majority with it; and let this portent of the world be deemed an eclipse of the sun, like others a portent only to the eye. Phlegon records

[21] ibid

[22] ibid

that, in the time of Tiberius Caesar, at full moon, there was a full eclipse of the sun from the sixth hour to the ninth—manifestly that one of which we speak. But what has an eclipse in common with an earthquake, the rending rocks, and the resurrection of the dead, and so great a perturbation throughout the universe? Surely no such event as this is recorded for a long period'.

Evidence 13: Jonathan Ben Uziel - Targum Jonathan

Targum Jonathan is a Targum (Targums are paraphrases, explanations and expansions of the Hebrew Bible from a Rabbi) which is attributed to Jonathan Ben Uziel (c 50 BC) by Talmudic (Talmud is a collection of writings of Jewish Rabbis) tradition. Targum Jonathan presents the following text[23] for the first 9 verses of Isaiah 53[24], a passage from the Hebrew Bible - '(1) Who hath believed this our report? and to whom is now the power of the arm of the Lord revealed? (2) The righteous shall be great before Him, behold, like branches that bud; and like a tree which sends forth its roots by the streams of water, thus shall the generation of the just multiply in the land, which hath need of Him. (3) His visage shall not be the visage of a common person, neither His fear the fear of a plebeian; but a holy brightness shall be His brightness, that every one who seeth Him shall contemplate Him. (4) Although He shall be in contempt; yet He shall cut off the glory of all the wicked, they shall be weak and wretched. Lo, we are in contempt and not esteemed, as a man of pain and appointed to sickness, and as if He had removed the face of His

[23] http://juchre.org/targums/isaiah/benisa.htm#53

[24] Isaiah 53 is understood to be text related to the Messiah, as even the Targum appreciates through the line 'Behold, my servant the Messiah shall prosper' (Targum on Isaiah 52:13) where 'the Messiah' is an addition in the Targum on top of the text in the Hebrew Bible.

Shekinah from us. (5) Therefore He shall pray for our sins, and our iniquities for His sake shall be forgiven us; for we are considered crushed, smitten of the Lord, and afflicted. (6) He shall build the house of the sanctuary, which has been profaned on account of our sins; He was delivered over on account of our iniquities, and through His doctrine peace shall be multiplied upon us, and through the teaching of His words our sins shall be forgiven us. (7) All we like sheep have been scattered, every one of us has turned to his own way; it pleased the Lord to forgive the sins of all of us for His sake. (8) He shall pray and He shall be answered, yea, before He shall open His mouth. He shall be heard; He shall deliver over the mighty of the nations as a lamb to the slaughter, and like a sheep before her shearers is dumb, none shall in His presence open his mouth, or speak a word. (9) He shall gather our captives from affliction and pain, and who shall be able to narrate the wonderful works which shall be done for us in His days? He shall remove the rule of the nations from the land of Israel, the sins which my people have committed have come upon them. (10) And He shall deliver the wicked into hell, and the riches of treasures which they got by violence unto the death of Abaddon, that they who commit sin shall not remain, and that they should not speak folly with their mouth. '

The writer of the Targum seems to have taken care in removing references to a 'suffering Messiah' who goes on to die, by drastically reinterpreting the text of the original Hebrew Bible. For instance, where a modern Jewish Publication Society (JPS) Bible translation states, 'He was despised, shunned by men, a man of suffering, familiar with disease … smitten and afflicted by God', the Targum states, 'Although He shall be in contempt; yet He shall cut off the glory of all the wicked, they shall be weak and wretched', making 'the wicked' to be the one who are 'weak' and 'wretched' as opposed to the Messiah being the 'man of suffering' and 'familiar with disease'. Similarly, where JPS Bible states, 'he was cut off from the land of the living' and 'his grave was set among the wicked', the Targum states 'He shall remove the rule of the nations from the land of Israel' and 'And He shall deliver the wicked into hell', making the 'nations' and the 'wicked' as the actual sufferers as opposed to the Messiah.

This is strong evidence to suggest that a school of thought the Messiah would not suffer and die certainly existed around the time of Jesus' life. In this context, the Gospels recording that Jews did not believe the Messiah would die, is reasonable (Element 6).

Summary - Extra-Biblical Evidences for the Crux of the Gospels

We have been able to comfortably establish most of the elements in the crux of the Gospels through the extra Biblical evidences that we have looked at. For the other elements, there is a reasonable case to be made through the evidences.

Table 7 - Elements of the Crux of the Gospels and Evidences

Element	Evidence
1 (Particular Jesus)	1, 2, 3, 5, 9
2 (Disciples)	1, 3, 4, 6
3 (Extravagant claims)	8
4 (New teaching)	3, 9

Element	Evidence
5 (Miracles)	3, 8, 9
6 (Dying Messiah - Alien Idea)	13
7 (Jewish leadership offended)	7, 9
8 (Jewish plan to destroy Jesus)	9
9 (Jewish accusation)	3, 9
10 (Roman condemnation)	1, 3
11 (Crucifixion)	3, 7, 9
12 (Nature's response to crucifixion)	10, 11, 12
13 (Disciples' belief in Jesus' resurrection)	1, 4, 6, 7
14 (Disciples worship Jesus)	4, 7, 8
15 (Persecution of the Early Church in Jerusalem)	1, 4, 7
16 (Growth of the Early Church in Jerusalem)	1

5. Is Jesus God?

We have come quite a distance now, from where we started. We have gone through information to convince ourselves that the text we have in the Gospels is 1st century text and that it is close enough to Jesus. Furthermore, we have also established that the content of the Gospels is historically reliable, first by establishing that the narration of the life of Jesus is firmly rooted in an accurate, historical context, and then by verifying that the crux of the narration has supporting evidence in various extra Biblical sources.

We might also, at this point, admit that we have been pretty harsh towards the Gospels so far, in our scrutiny of establishing their reliability, because we have, so far, treated the Gospels as if they were 'guilty until proven innocent'. It could be said that, arguably, no historical artefact has been subjected to as much hostile and harsh evaluation as the Gospels have been. Thankfully, despite our harshness, the Gospels have withstood the intense scrutiny, and have prevailed.

In our harsh treatment so far, we have been able to establish the following. Firstly, the early disciples held on to their belief of Jesus being divine (Elements 13 and 14) despite severe persecution (Element 15). Secondly, even after the persecution started (Element 15), despite Jewish inclination to think that their Christ would not die (Element 6) and despite becoming objects of the persecution, there were many people who were convinced about the claims about Jesus that they became new disciples of him who had just died (Element 16).

As we might appreciate, holding onto one's belief, despite knowledge of a clear threat to life because of the belief, and despite having the ability to relinquish the belief and avoid the threat and in the absence of any clear benefit that comes from outside of the belief, is perhaps the best test of strength of the person's belief. We have established that the early disciples had demonstrated this strength in their beliefs concerning Jesus. Their beliefs might include simple observations and complex conclusions. Their demonstration of the strength of their beliefs meań they were convinced both about their simple observations and complex conclusions. We wouldn't have to take their complex conclusions at their word, but we must admit that, given their willingness even to face persecution for their beliefs, we must take them as reliable witnesses for their simple observations. Using these simple observations as building blocks, we might then see for ourselves, if their complex conclusions are logically sound.

As you could see this step in our scrutiny involves initially figuring out their simple observations (and taking them as reliable building blocks), understanding their rationale to come to their complex conclusions and then finally concluding for ourselves if their conclusions are rational and evidential. Guiding questions for us could be - Why did the early disciples spread belief in Jesus, after his death, despite persecution? Why did new disciples become disciples, right in Jerusalem, despite persecution and despite not expecting a dying Messiah?

Gospels as the Official Early Disciples' Account of Jesus

Now that we have decided that we are going to place the early disciples in the dock and get to know their simple observations so that we could verify if their complex conclusions about Jesus are rational and evidential, the point to be established is that the 4 Gospels namely Matthew, Mark, Luke and John, along with the Acts of the Apostles (or just Acts) are the official testimony accounts of the early disciples about Jesus and themselves.

Internal Evidence

The Gospels and the Acts of the Apostles, in some cases explicitly, but largely implicitly through their narration, claim a great of degree of insider view of the life of Jesus and the early disciples, to the prudent reader.

The Gospels give details which might only be available to someone who is in close company with Jesus - timing of one specific instance of Jesus leaving Judea to Galilee [Matt 4:12; Mark 1:14; Luke 4:14; John 4:1-4:4], Jesus healing a specific person of a specific ailment [Matt 8:14-8:17; Mark 1:29-1:34; Luke 4:38-4:41], Jesus having dinner at a specific person's place [Matt 9:9-9:13; Mark 2:13-2:17; Luke 5:27-5:32] etc. This list of examples could actually be extended to cover the entire life of Jesus. This either tells us that the Gospel writers had either first hand information or had reasonable access to people with first hand information.

Two of the Gospels - Luke and John - make explicit claims about their writers being intimately connected to the life of Jesus and the early disciples.

The writer of the book of Luke suggests that events in Jesus' life were fulfilled in the neighbourhood of his company [Luke 1:1] and that he had 'perfect understanding of all things from the very first' [Luke 1:3]. Whether he himself was an eyewitness isn't crystal clear from his expression 'those who from the beginning were eyewitnesses and ministers of the word delivered them to us' [Luke 1:2] (especially because of the use of the 'those'), even though an argument could be made for it. In any case, at the least he was in the very vicinity of the life of Jesus, as it unfolded, and had rich access to eyewitnesses, which he could use in his account.

The writer of the book of John [John 21:24] claims that he was very close to Jesus, to an extent he was even leaning on Jesus during the last supper [John 21:20], and that he was uniquely qualified to be even uniquely identified as 'the disciple whom Jesus loved' [John 21:20]. As if this were not enough, the rest of the close disciples of Jesus seem to vouch for the contents of this Gospel [John 21:24].

Cross Evidence

The 4 Gospels were written by different writers (perhaps at different points in time). This is evident from the fact that each of them exhibit a reasonably unique literary style, even though the genre of their content are broadly comparable. Furthermore, each of them, to serve their purpose to highlight specific aspects of Jesus' life, use different sets of events in Jesus' life.

Despite these differences, what is remarkable is that all 4 Gospels are perfectly in unison in their details about Jesus' life, when examined carefully, thereby authenticating the credibility of each other as being testimonies of people close to Jesus. This unison is an interesting subject area in itself with J.J. Blunt producing 34 'undesigned coincidences' that he brings up in one of his works[25] to ascertain the authenticity of the Gospels.

[25] 'Undesigned Coincidences in the Writings of the Old and New Testament - An Argument of their Veracity' - J. J. Blunt.

External Evidence

Extra Biblical writings of Christian leaders such as Ignatius of Antioch (died c. AD 110), Polycarp of Smyrna (c. AD 70 - c. AD 155), Justin Martyr (c. AD 100 - c. AD 165), Irenaeus of Lyons (c. AD 120/140 - c. AD 202), Clement of Alexandria (c. AD 150 - c. AD 212), Tertullian of Carthage (c. AD 155 - c. AD 220) and others use distinctive quotations that seem to have been borrowed from the 4 Gospels.

Muratorian Canon is a document that lists the 4 Gospels, Matthew, Mark, Luke and John as the only authoritative Gospels, and the book of Acts as the only authoritative account of the Apostles' acts, used among Christians. Apart from the Gospels and Acts it goes on to list other authoritative books of the New Testament also. The content of this list is dated to, latest, end of 2nd century.

Summary

Gospels namely Matthew, Mark, Luke and John, along with the book of Acts seem to be the only documents which were accepted as authoritative narration of the life of Jesus and the early disciples (especially Apostles). We could therefore confidently use these documents as the authoritative documents to get information about Jesus, his disciples and their beliefs. It is for the information that these documents provide that the early disciples were willing to even lay down their lives. Appendix B has a note on the Gospels which are not considered part of the authoritative list of Gospels.

Categories of Early Disciples

So far, we had seen the early disciples as one homogenous group. Even though, in many ways they proved themselves to be homogenous, their own testimonies reveal that not everyone had similar exposure to Jesus. There are broadly 3 categories of early disciples - thorough eyewitnesses, inner circle and others.

Thorough Eyewitnesses (Including the Twelve)

Jesus, during the course of his ministry had chosen twelve disciples whom he had chosen and appointed as Apostles (official emissaries) [Matt 10:2-10:4; Mark 3:13-3:19; Luke 6:12-6:16]. These twelve were chosen so that 'they might be with Him' [Mark 3:14-3:15], presumably so they could be eyewitnesses of all things and learn all things from him. One of these, Judas, later betrayed Jesus. He subsequently committed suicide [Matt 27:3-27:10] and was not part of the early disciples who were persecuted. There were a number of other disciples also, who like the Apostles, had accompanied Jesus all the time [Acts 1:21]. These people could be categorised as 'thorough eyewitnesses' of relevant details of Jesus' life, within reasonable limits. By no means, did they claim to have tagged onto Jesus, literally 'all through' his public ministry. Rather, they had been with Jesus to witness all relevant teachings and works of Jesus.

Inner Circle

Even though the category of people given above, 'thorough eyewitnesses', were eyewitnesses of all relevant teachings and works of Jesus, 3 among the 12 Apostles, Simon Peter, James and John (the latter 2 were nicknamed Boanerges [Mark 3:17]) were witnesses to 3 special events in Jesus' life. These 3 were the only close eyewitnesses of a miracle where

Jesus raised a dead young girl back to life [Mark 5:37; Luke 8:51], transfiguration of Jesus [Matt 17:1; Mark 9:2; Luke 9:28] and Jesus' prayer in the Garden of Gethsemane [Matt 26:37; Mark 14:33]. These 3 are popularly called the 'inner circle' of disciples. There is no explicit claim in the Gospels about why Jesus had an inner circle.

Others

Apart from the thorough eyewitnesses and the inner circle, there were many other disciples that Jesus had within a couple of months after the supposed resurrection. For instance, Acts 1:15 mentions that there were about 120 disciples gathered together with Simon Peter (one of the 'inner circle'). Furthermore, about 3000 became new disciples after Simon Peter's first public preaching after the supposed resurrection [Acts 2:41].

Jesus had raised a team of 70 witnesses in his last year in public ministry [Luke 10:1-10:24]. Whether these 70 were thorough eyewitnesses or not, we could not be sure. At the least they could be considered as partial eyewitnesses.

It is possible that some of the other disciples in this category were other partial eyewitnesses of Jesus' teachings and works. Jesus had many such partial eyewitnesses who had 'followed' him at different points in time and had witnessed some part of his teachings and works. This includes the multitude who had witnessed Jesus in Galilee [Matt 12:15-21; Mark 3:7-12; Luke 6:17-19] and in Judea [John 7:31]. Some of these partial eyewitnesses even get a special mention in the Gospels. A couple of examples are - a centurion whose servant was healed [Matt 8:5-8:13; Luke 7:1-7:10], a nobleman whose son was healed by Jesus [John 4:46-4:54] and another centurion who had witnessed special events during crucifixion [Matt 27:51-27:56; Mark 15:38-15:41; Luke 23:45; 23:47-23:49].

It is also possible that some of the other disciples in this category were from a group of 500 who had witnessed Jesus, while they were together, after his supposed resurrection. James, Jesus' half brother was also one of Jesus' early disciples, becoming a disciple soon after resurrection [1 Corinthians 15:6-7].

Simple Observations of the Early Disciples

The insider experience of the early disciples have a few important elements, from the disciples' interaction with Jesus, which could be deemed to be 'simple observations'. These are called 'simple observations' because they could be 'observed' using one of their senses 'straight away' without having to have much knowledge outside of the ordinary experiences in life. An example of a simple observation could be witnessing two people talking to each other. Simple observations could also be a bit more complex, but still could be called simple. For instance, even if a dead man were to be raised back to life, as long as one has some experience of knowing when someone is dead and when someone is alive, and as long as he had witnessed the entire process of the man being dead through to the man being raised back to life, his experience could be categorised as 'simple observation', because incredible as the event might sound, he witnessed the entire process and could vouch for it. Of course, the only catch in this definition is that we expect the witness to be sane and with decent physical potential to witness, which we would expect out of any witness of any event anyway. Some such 'simple observations' of the early disciples are listed below. These formed the foundation blocks of the early disciples coming to 'complex conclusions' about Jesus.

Element 1 (Recap): Particular Jesus (Witness: Public)

The name 'Jesus' (in its Hebrew form) is a very popular Jewish name, especially in the 1st century. The name 'James' (a half-brother of Jesus) is also another very popular Jewish name. However, the Jesus of the Gospels, who had a half brother called James could be uniquely identified by the title that was attributed to him in the Gospels, namely - Messiah or Christ.

Element 3 (Recap): Extravagant Claims (Witness: Public)

The particular Jesus of the Gospels, even by Jewish standards of bold claims made by various prophets, had many bold, public claims attributed to himself. For instance, he was claimed to be Son of God [Matt 3:16-3:17; Mark 1:10-1:11; Luke 1:35; Luke 3:22; John 1:32-1:34], One greater than the Temple [Matt 12:6], Lord of the Sabbath [Matt 12:8; Mark 2:28; Luke 6:5], someone who was one with the Jewish God [John 10:30], teacher [Matt 19:16; Mark 10:17; Luke 18:18; John 20:16], prophet [Matt 13:57; Mark 6:4; John 4:44] and king [Matt 27:11; Mark 15:2; Luke 23:3; John 18:36].

Element 5a: Supernatural Power (Witness: Public)

Jesus, through his miracles, demonstrated power over various entities. He demonstrated power over human infirmities [Matt 12:9-12:14; Mark 3:1-3:6; Luke 6:6-6:11; John 5:1-5:47], death [Matt 9:18-9:26; Mark 5:21-5:43; Luke 8:40-8:56; John 11:1-11:44], material things [Matt 14:13-14:21; Mark 6:30-6:44; Luke 9:10-9:17; John 6:1-6:14], sin [Matt 9:1-9:8; Mark 2:1-2:12; Luke 5:17-5:26] and spiritual forces (demons) [Matt 12:22-12:37; Mark 3:20-3:30; Luke 11:14-11:23].

Of particular note among all the miracles was the raising up of Lazarus back to life, after he had been dead for 4 days [John 11:1-11:44]. This sign is somewhat special because of the timing, place and people involved. This miracle was performed in Bethany, reasonably close to Jerusalem epicentre of attendance during Jewish feasts, just a few weeks before Passover, right about the time when people who visit Jerusalem for the Passover show up in Jerusalem. Furthermore, many who had opposed Jesus in his ministry seem to have known Lazarus and family and therefore were very aware of the death and were in attendance to witness the resurrection.

All these signs are considered as 'simple observations' because they were witnessed uninterrupted. In other words, witnesses had without much deviation, seen the states of 'before the miracle', 'during the miracle' and 'after the miracle'.

Element 5b: Supernatural Power (Witness: Thorough Eyewitnesses & Inner Circle)

The thorough eyewitnesses and the inner circle had seen all the miracles that Jesus had done in public to demonstrate his power. On top of these miracles, they were also witnesses to some events which demonstrated power over material things [John 2:1-2:11] and nature [Matt 8:23-8:27; Mark 4:35-4:41; Luke 8:22-8:25].

These signs are considered as 'simple observations' because they were witnessed uninterrupted. In other words, witnesses had without much deviation, seen the states of 'before the miracle', 'during the miracle' and 'after the miracle'.

Element 6 (Recap): Dying Messiah - An Alien Idea (Witness: Public)

Even towards the end of Jesus' time in public ministry, the Jews hadn't expected that their true Messiah (Christ) would die [John 12:34].

Element 8 (Recap): Jewish Plan to Destroy Jesus (Witness: Public)

Jewish leadership had planned to destroy Jesus much ahead of the actual crucifixion. The Pharisees and the Herodians had planned to destroy him perhaps more than a year before the actual crucifixion [Matt 12:14; Mark 3:6; Luke 6:11], but all of Jewish leadership agreed to destroy him perhaps a few weeks before the actual crucifixion [John 11:45-11:54].

Element 17a: Voice From Heaven (Witness: Public)

Multitudes that were around Jesus in one instance heard a voice from heaven speak to Jesus [John 12:28]. Some remarked that it had thundered while some others that an angel had spoken to Jesus [John 12:29].

Element 17b: Voice From Heaven (Witness: Inner Circle)

On top of hearing a voice from heaven speaking to Jesus, in public [John 12:28], the inner circle had also heard a voice from heaven instructing them that Jesus was his beloved Son and that they had to hear him [Matt 17:5; Mark 9:7; Luke 9:35]. The voice, owing to the origin, was quite rightly adjudged to be that of God by the witnesses.

Element 18: Transfiguration (Witness: Inner Circle)

At one specific point in time, in the sight of the inner circle, Jesus was transfigured and his face shone like the sun and his clothes as white as the light [Matt 17:1-17:13; Mark 9:2-9:13; Luke 9:28-9:36].

Element 9 (Recap): Jewish Accusation (Witness: Public)

Jewish leadership during Jesus' time were instrumental in getting Jesus condemned to capital punishment [Matt 27:12; Mark 15:14; Luke 23:21; John 19:6].

Element 10 (Recap): Roman Condemnation (Witness: Public)

Jesus was condemned to be crucified by Roman prefect Pontius Pilate [Matt 27:24; Mark 15:15; Luke 23:24; John 19:16]

Element 11 (Recap): Crucifixion (Witness: Public)

Jesus was executed by crucifixion [Matt 20:19; Mark 15:15; Luke 23:21; Luke 23:24; John 19:16]

Element 12 (Recap): Nature's Response to Crucifixion (Witness: Public)

There was darkness for 3 hours at midday during Jesus' crucifixion [Matt 27:45; Mark 15:33; Luke 23:44], the earth quaked and rocks split [Matt 27:51].

Element 19: Appearance of Dead Saints (Witness: Public)

During the crucifixion, graves were opened and many bodies of Jewish saints who were dead were raised. They came out of their graves after His resurrection and went into Jerusalem and appeared to many [Matt 27:52-27:53].

Element 20: Death, Burial and Sealed Tomb (Witness: Public)

Jesus was adjudged as dead [Mark 15:44-15:45] by expert Roman executioners, through means verified to be valid by modern medical professionals [John 19:31-19:37]. He was then buried in a tomb owned by a Jewish leader (Joseph of Arimathea) who was part of the council that had recommended that Jesus be crucified and Nicodemus, a teacher of the Jews [Matt 27:57-27:60; Mark 15:42-15:46; Luke 23:50-23:54; John 19:38-19:42]. Some of the women disciples had noted where Jesus was buried [Matt 27:61; Mark 15:47; Luke 23:55-23:56]. The tomb was later sealed by a Roman guard [Matt 27:62-27:66].

Element 21: Empty Tomb (Witness: Public)

The tomb which was under Roman guard, where Jesus was buried on a Friday evening, was found open and empty on Sunday morning. The empty tomb was first witnessed by a few women disciples (including Mary Magdalene) [Matt 28:8; Mark 16:8; Luke 24:3; Luke 24:9-24:11] and later on by Peter and the writer of the Gospel of John [Luke 24:12; John 20:2-20:10].

Element 22: Post Burial Appearances (Witness: Thorough Witnesses and Inner Circle)

After the empty tomb was witnessed, Jesus showed up to many people in different occasions - Mary Magdalene [Mark 16:9; Beloved 20:14-20:17], a few women [Matt 28:9-28:10], Cleopas and Simon [Mark 16:12-16:13; Luke 24:13-24:35] and many disciples (including the eleven surviving Apostles) [Mark 16:14; Luke 24:36-24:43; Beloved 20:19-20:25] amongst other appearances. Finally, Jesus also ascended up into heaven [Mark 16:19-16:20; Luke 24:50-24:53].

Element 23: Jesus' Clarification on the Messianic Prophecies

In the context of Jews not expecting their true Messiah (Christ) to die, Jesus opened up the Jewish scriptures and explained to the disciples that the Messiah had to suffer and die and then rise again [Luke 24:44-24:49].

Element 24: Miracles Performed by Apostles After Jesus' Ascension (Witness: Public)

The Apostles themselves, after Jesus' ascension performed many signs and wonders [Mark 16:20; Acts 2:43].

Evaluating Early Disciples' Complex Conclusions

Let us reiterate some things which we have clearly laid out before. We have established that the early disciples had demonstrated a certain strength in their beliefs concerning Jesus through their willingness to be persecuted for their beliefs. The demonstration of the strength of their beliefs means they were convinced both about their simple observations and complex conclusions. They should be held as reliable witnesses of their simple observations, without any question. Where they need to be scrutinised is in evaluating if their 'complex conclusions' were rational and evidential.

Jesus' Supernatural Power

Jesus, right through 3 years of public life demonstrated his supernatural power (Elements 5a and 5b). Apart from a handful of times (Element 5b), the remaining recorded miracles were done in public (Element 5a). The Gospels also clarify that Jesus had performed far more miracles than what had been listed in the Gospels [Matt 4:23-4:25; Mark 1:35-1:39; Luke 4:42-4:44]. Even in the last few hours before Jesus' death on the cross tremendous evidences (simple observations) were offered to indicate that Jesus had supernatural power (Elements 12 and 19).

For followers and sceptics of Jesus alike, that he had supernatural power was never in doubt. They had come to this conclusion based on 'simple observations'. People responded to his miracles with comments such as - 'for with authority and power He commands the unclean spirits, and they come out' [Mark 1:21-1:28; Luke 4:31-4:37], 'a great prophet has risen up among us and, God has visited His people.' [Luke 7:11-7:17], 'it was never seen like this in Israel!' [Matt 9:32-9:34] and 'He has done all things well. He makes both the deaf to hear and the mute to speak' [Matt 15:29-15:31; Mark 7:31-7:37].

What was a 'complex conclusion' to them, based on the simple observations of the miracles, was the exact source of the supernatural power of Jesus. Some considered Jesus to have acquired his supernatural power from evil forces [Matt 12:22-12:37; Mark 3:20-3:30]. Some perceived him to be a great prophet of God (and therefore having supernatural power endowed by God) who was prophesied about in the Hebrew Bible [Matt 14:13-14:21; Mark 6:30-6:44; Luke 9:10-9:17; John 6:1-6:14]. Some considered him good and some others considered him a deceiver [John 7:2, 7:11-7:52]. About midway through Jesus' public life, even the thorough witnesses of Jesus were still working out to understand who exactly Jesus was because they saw supernatural power which was even beyond the reach of the Jewish prophets of God [Matt 8:23-8:27; Mark 4:35-4:41; Luke 8:22-8:25].

That Jesus had demonstrated supernatural power was also evident through Evidences 8 and 9. There is no evidence contrary to the idea that Jesus was a miracles-performer.

With all these witness statements for the fact of Jesus demonstrating supernatural power consistently and throughout his public life, it would be imprudent of us to defy it as irrational and non-evidential.

Resolution of Jesus' Identity

After Jesus had demonstrated his supernatural power quite consistently (Elements 5a and 5b), the only area left to 'interpretation' of the witnesses, for some period, was the precise identity of Jesus; more precisely the question of whether he was of God or not. During this period, after many events, when Jesus had demonstrated his ability to feed people supernaturally (just like how the God of Israel had fed Israel in Mosaic times), and followed that up by walking on water, the disciples, who had the Jewish history as a backdrop, had assessed that Jesus was 'truly the Son of God' [Matt 14:22-14:33; Mark 6:45-6:52; John 6:15-6:21]. Sometime later, Simon Peter (one of Jesus' inner circle) had made a confession based on his experience with Jesus, that Jesus was 'Christ, the Son of the living God' [Matt 16:13-16:20; Mark 8:27-8:30; Luke 9:18-9:21]. This complex conclusion of Jesus being the son of God might not strike a chord with those who might not know enough of the history of Israel to trust the validity of this conclusion.

Jesus had been introduced [John 1:29-1:34] and had introduced himself [John 2:13-2:22] as the Christ, the Son of God (Elements 1 and 3). These introductions were clearly witnessed in public (simple observations). Prior to Jesus' supposed resurrection, there were some simple observations which provided reasons to agree with this introduction. The inner circle saw Jesus transfigured (Element 18) and also heard from heaven a supernatural voice clearly communicating that Jesus was indeed who he claimed to be (Element 17b). General public also, at another instance, heard a voice from heaven communicating to Jesus (Element 17a). Add to this, nature's response and unprecedented supernatural resurrections at the time of Jesus' death (Elements 12 and 19). When Elements 1, 3, 17a, 17b, 18 are put together, the only logical conclusion would be to consider Jesus to be who he really claimed himself to be - Christ, the Son of God.

Jesus' Resurrection

Resurrection (Jesus coming back to life after he was dead) is the simplest and most reasonable 'complex' conclusion that could be drawn from the simple observations - Elements 20, 21 and 22.

The complex conclusion of resurrection could be refuted only if at least one of Elements 20, 21 and 22 is undermined.

There are only a few possibilities of undermining Element 20.

As one of the alternative theories which has been advanced many times in the past claims, Jesus perhaps never died on the cross, but merely fell unconscious but later was revived (swoon theory). Another alternative theory is to perhaps suggest that the body of Jesus was not buried where it was thought to have buried.

These alternative theories seriously undermine some 'basic' things. Firstly, they call to question the capability of the world's best army at that time, the Roman army in both 'killing' a crucified person and providing a guard to him right through the crucifixion to burial when needed (Element 11). Secondly, this mocks the best administration apparatus of that time, which was perhaps much better than most of the modern day Governments (if not all of them), the Roman administration (Elements 10 and 11). This Roman administration crucified Jesus under Roman guard and had tracked this issue seriously to appease the Jewish leadership (Element 9). Thirdly, this undermines the rigorousness with which the Jewish leadership was pursuing the 'issue' of Jesus (Elements 8 and 9) as established through Evidences 3 and 9. Fourthly, this fails to answer the question of how the disciples would have become willing to be persecuted (Element 15) if at least some of them hadn't seen him dead in the first place, before he was buried.

Element 21 is really binary - either the tomb was empty or it wasn't. If we assume the tomb was not empty but was believed to be empty or was lied about being empty, we are essentially undermining a few things again. It doesn't explain why disciples would be willing to be persecuted if at least some of them hadn't really seen the tomb to be empty (Element 15). Also, this goes against the intention of Jewish leadership to deal with the 'issue' of Jesus. The 'issue' of Jesus would still remain if Jesus was believed to have vacated his tomb, when he was really inside the tomb. In this case, to further their intention (Elements 8 and 9), they would have just (perhaps with the Roman administration apparatus and Roman guard) brought to the attention of the general public, the fact that Jesus' body was still resting in the tomb, and quenched the growth of the church (Element 16).

Element 22 has been contested in a couple of different ways in the past.

One alternative offered is that perhaps the disciples never witnessed any appearances of Jesus after his death; they had just lied. There are a few major problems with this alternative. Firstly, it fails to explain why disciples who were deliberately lying would be willing to give up their lives for this lie during the persecution of the church (Element 16).

Secondly, merely lying would not make a body vanish away from its tomb. The body under the protection of the expert Roman guard should have still been in the tomb and the zealous Jewish leadership should have quelled the 'issue' of Jesus once and for all by merely displaying the body of Jesus to everyone and exposing the lies of the disciples.

Another alternative is that perhaps disciples were genuinely merely hallucinating (hallucination theory). They truly saw something - but what they had seen wasn't a 'real' Jesus but rather was an 'illusory' Jesus. There are a few problems with this alternative also. Firstly, similar to the previous alternative, merely hallucinating would not make a body vanish away from its tomb. The body under the protection of the expert Roman guard should have still been in the tomb and the zealous Jewish leadership should have quelled the 'issue' of Jesus once and for all by merely displaying the body of Jesus to everyone and exposing the fantasies of the disciples. Secondly, it fails to give a viable route to justify this alternative given that different groups of people in different circumstances witnessed post burial appearances of Jesus (as explained in Element 22).

The alternative theories suggested to undermine 'simple observations', Elements 20, 21 and 22 are fraught with issues. Each one of them seriously fail to fit well with the entire gamut of observations which have been backed by extra Biblical sources also. Resurrection seems like the most straightforward 'complex conclusion' of all that seamlessly brings together Elements 20, 21 and 22. The disciples' belief in resurrection, therefore, would be reasonable and evidential.

Summary

Based on the facts around the 'simple observations', the disciples 'complex conclusions' about the person of Jesus seem to be reasonable and evidential and are the most straightforward of all explanations available to explain the 'simple observations'.

Jesus, who clearly demonstrated supernatural power, was justified to be an authority of over life and death, through his resurrection. Furthermore, he was clearly communicated to be 'Christ, the son of God' equal to God (as per Jesus' claim to be 'the One greater than the Temple', 'the Lord of the Sabbath' and someone who was 'one with God').

The Growth of the Early Church Despite Persecution

The 'simple observations' that the disciples had and their 'complex conclusions' which we have now established to be reasonable and evidential provide a coherent view of the history of the very early Church.

The inner circle, other thorough eyewitnesses and others were consistently exposed to the supernatural power that was at work through Jesus (Elements 1, 3, 5a and 5b). Skeptics of Jesus, had at this stage sowed in confusion about the origin of the supernatural power. While the general population had to grapple with the 2 views in contention, the inner circle and the other thorough eyewitnesses were given a precise understanding of who Jesus was, through supernatural revelations (Elements 17a, 17b and 18). These supernatural revelations gave them a theoretical framework to back up their practical commitment to following Jesus, despite the oncoming persecution.

Jewish religious authorities, noticing Jesus' growing popularity decided to have him destroyed (Element 8). They eventually had Jesus accused (Element 9) and crucified (Element 11) through the approval of the Roman authorities (Element 10). The disciples who had not really prepared themselves well to deal with a dying Christ (Element 6) had found the death of Jesus difficult to handle, despite the supernatural events during the crucifixion (Element 12 and 19).

It was in this difficult juncture, when the disciples had to deal with the death of Jesus, that resurrection came as a way forward (Elements 20, 21 and 22). The resurrected Jesus clarified to the disciples that Christ had to die (Element 23) and gave the disciples a clear insight of the events until that point. The resurrection and the clarification about the need for Christ to die strengthened the disciples to stand up and testify boldly, right in Jerusalem, where they had been downcast, a few weeks ago. The testimony of the early disciples was backed up by the many miracles that the Apostles themselves did in Jerusalem (Element 24). This testimony, backed up by the miracles that the Apostles performed, enabled the others (many of whom were likely to be at least partial eyewitnesses of Jesus) to be convicted about belief in Jesus and enabled them to decide to become his disciples also.

6. Conclusion

It might seem as if we have come almost to the end of a very exhilarating scrutiny experience. Sure - it would be right to seem so.

We have now established that the Gospels are reliable accounts of history concerning Jesus. We have also established that the disciples of Jesus were reasonable in their consideration of Jesus as Christ and God.

However, the truth of the matter is, the truly exhilarating part begins just now. Let us take a step back and carefully think about this. What we really have established so far is that it is quite rational to consider that Jesus was the creator of all things both large and small. The vast Universe out there with the innumerable number of heavenly bodies - Jesus created all of them. The microscopic, yet very sophisticated engineering and biological marvels that we see in various living cells - Jesus created them too. It is this Jesus who is the reason of your existence and my existence, who really took a stroll in the midst of human history. But for what?

Now we return back to what the many Christians have always been telling us. No one puts it clearer than Jesus himself. His prime message when he was on Earth was this - "The time is fulfilled, and the kingdom of God is at hand. Repent, and believe in the gospel." [Mark 1:15]. Jesus had come into the world to usher in what was rightly called the kingdom of God. The very kingdom which was designed originally by God, for man to enjoy, under the kingship of God. Unfortunately though, for various reasons, throughout time, men have wandered off from this kingdom, for the sake of really silly, irrational and false pleasures such as the lust of the flesh, the lust of the eyes and the pride of life. God in his gentle mercy towards man though, wants us back on track.

The ones who are already weary of the things of this world Jesus invites - 'Come to Me, all you who labor and are heavy laden, and I will give you rest. Take My yoke upon you and learn from Me, for I am gentle and lowly in heart, and you will find rest for your souls. For My yoke is easy and My burden is light.' [Matt 11:28-11:30]. The ones who have come to their wits end and realise that there is no real life Jesus invites - 'If anyone thirsts, let him come to Me and drink. He who believes in Me, as the Scripture has said, out of his heart will flow rivers of living water' [John 7:37-7:38]. Jesus' admonition though, is quite clear - he wants us to 'repent, and believe' in what he has to offer. He wants us to take the steps that we could take to seek after the real life, which is in him. He says - 'Labour for the food that endures to everlasting life' [John 6:27]. The ball, however, is in our court. How are we going to respond to him?

Responding to Pilate, during his trial, Jesus said - 'You say rightly that I am a king. For this cause I was born, and for this cause I have come into the world, that I should bear witness to the truth. Everyone who is of the truth hears My voice.' [John 18:37]. Question is – are we of the truth?

Further Reading

Biographies of Jesus

1. The Book of Matthew
2. The Book of Mark
3. The Book of Luke
4. The Book of John

Manuscripts of the New Testament

1. The Text of the New Testament: Its Transmission, Corruption, and Restoration, Third, Enlarged Edition, Bruce M. Metzger
2. The New Testament Documents: Are They Reliable? F. F. Bruce
3. The Books and the Parchments: How We Got Our English Bible, F. F. Bruce
4. http://csntm.org/

Textual Variants

1. http://bible.ovc.edu/tc/index.htm
2. http://prototypes.openscriptures.org/manuscript-comparator/

New Testament Canon

1. The Canon of the New Testament: Its Origin, Development, and Significance, Bruce M. Metzger
2. The Canon of Scripture, F. F. Bruce
3. http://www.ntcanon.org/

Jesus in Extra Biblical Sources

1. Jesus and Christian Origins Outside the New Testament, F. F. Bruce
2. Jesus Outside the New Testament: An Introduction to the Ancient Evidence (Studying the Historical Jesus), Robert E. Van Voorst
3. The Historical Jesus: Ancient Evidence for the Life of Christ, Gary R. Habermas
4. Jesus Under Fire: Modern Scholarship Reinvents the Historical Jesus, Ed. by Michael J. Wilkins and J. P. Moreland
5. Christianity: The Witness of History, Norman Anderson
6. Gospel Perspectives, Volume 5: The Jesus Tradition Outside the Gospels, Ed. by David Wenham
7. 'Did Jesus Exist? Searching for Evidence Beyond the Bible', Lawrence Mykytiuk, www.biblicalarchaeology.org, 18/11/2015

Resurrection of Jesus

1. The Resurrection of Jesus: A New Historiographical Approach, Michael R. Licona
2. 'The Resurrection of Jesus', William Lane Craig, http://www.reasonablefaith.org, 03/12/2015
3. Riddle of Resurrection: "Dying and Rising Gods" in the Ancient Near East, Tryggve N. D. Mettinger

Appendices

A. Historicity of the Book of Acts (Acts of the Apostles)

The Book of Acts (Acts of the Apostles) is a historical narrative on the early Church from the time of Jesus' ascension. It is the only work on the 1st century disciples of Jesus recognized to be official by the early disciples.

Table A.1 - Uncial Manuscripts of the book of Acts from first 5 Centuries

Identifier	Name	Time	Comment
א	Codex Sinaiticus, British Library, London, UK	4th century	Acts
A	Codex Alexandrinus, British Library, London, UK	5th century	Acts
B	Codex Vaticanus, Vatican Library, Vatican City	Middle 4th century	Acts apart from a few verses
C	Codex Ephraemi (Palimpsest), Bibliothèque nationale de France, Paris, France	5th century	Portions of Acts
D	Codex Bezae, Cambridge University Library, Cambridge, UK	5th/6th century	Most of Acts

Table A.2 - Papyrus Fragments for Acts (First 3 Centuries)

Identifier	Name	Time	Verses (Acts)
P^{29}	P. Oxy. 1597; Gr. bibl. g. 4 (P), Bodleian Library, Oxford, UK	AD 250	26
P^{45}	BP I, Chester Beatty Library, Dublin, Ireland	AD 250	4-17
P^{48}	PSI 1165, Laurentian Library, Florence, Italy	AD 250	23
P^{53}	Inv. 6652, University of Michigan, Michigan, US	AD 250	9-10
P^{91}	P. Mil. Vofl. Inv. 1224, Università degli Studi di Milano, Milan, Italy and P. Macquarie inv. 360, Macquarie University, Sydney, Australia	AD 250	2:30-37; 2:46-3:2
P^{38}	P. Mich. 138; Inv. 1571, University of Michigan, Michigan, US	AD 300	18-19
P^{50}	P. 1543, Yale University Library, Connecticut, US	AD 300	8-10

B. A Note on Rejected Gospels

The purpose of a biography is to paint a picture (figuratively) of a person in a reasonable level of detail. In order to do this, the biographer must have or acquire intimate knowledge of the subject of the biography. Even if they claim to have intimate knowledge, their work might be scrutinized by both contemporaries to the subject and later experts, to see if it is an accurate depiction of the subject and the historical context.

In the case of the historical Jesus, we have already established certain conclusions about the Gospels namely Matthew, Mark, Luke and John. In Chapter 3, we established that these Gospels are, based on documentary evidence, close to the historical Jesus and therefore are very good candidates for being accurate depictions of Jesus. In Chapter 4, we established that the crux of the Gospels is corroborated by various extra-Biblical sources. In Chapter 5, we established that these Gospels were recognized to be accurate portrayal of Jesus by Jesus' early disciples.

In the last century, there are various documents which have been unearthed, which are widely used to advance some sensational stories about Jesus, which are not attested by the Gospels of Matthew, Mark, Luke and John. Whether these documents were meant to be taken as authentic works or not by their writers themselves is unclear in some cases. However, this does not stop those who want to use these works to advance sensational stories about Jesus.

Serious scholarly works on these documents conclusively discredit a majority of these documents and cast legitimate doubts about the remaining on various grounds, and rightly categorize these works as Apocrypha (from a Greek adjective which means 'obscure').

Gnostic Text on Jesus

From the 2nd to 4th centuries AD, a movement known as 'Gnosticism' centred in Egypt advanced an idea that spiritual attainment was related to a certain 'enlightenment' that could be derived from some hidden teachings. This movement made use of Jesus to advance their ideas.

This movement and its writings are localised to Egypt (geographically distant to Israel) and are dated to much after the time of the contemporary eyewitnesses of Jesus. Furthermore, they were not alone not positively attested by the early Christian community, but in many cases were explicitly pointed out for disapproval as being not accurate in their depiction of Jesus and his teachings as known to his disciples with roots in Israel.

Sayings Gospel of Thomas, Gospel of Judas (Iscariot), Gospel of Mary (Magdalene), Gospel of Philip, Greek Gospel of the Egyptians, Gospel of Truth, Pistis Sophia, Second Treatise of the Great Seth and Coptic Gospel of the Egyptians are some prominent Gnostic texts on Jesus.

Infancy Gospels

There are a few documents which purport to give details about Jesus' infancy (and in some cases, Jesus' parents' early lives). Infancy Gospel of James, Infancy Gospel of Thomas, Gospel of Pseudo Matthew, Syriac Infancy Gospel, History of Joseph the Carpenter and Life of John the Baptist are some of these works. These works do not contradict the crux of the Gospels of Matthew, Mark, Luke and John that we have established in Chapters 4 and 5. However, these Gospels are fraught with issues such as late origin, inaccurate descriptions of Jewish customs, stylistically unrelated to purported writers and are geographically separated from Israel.

Jewish Gospels

Gospel of Ebionites, Gospel of the Hebrews and Gospel of Nazarenes are prominent Jewish Christian Gospels. All of these were late in origin.

Passion Gospels

Gospel of Peter, Gospel of Nicodemus / Acts of Pilate, On the life of and the passion of Christ, Gospel of Bartholomew, Questions of Bartholomew, Resurrection of Jesus Christ are all gospels which are late in origin and are dubious in their claims of authorship. They were not regarded as representative of early witness testimonies about Jesus.

Harmonized Gospels

Diatessaron by Tatian is a late synthesis of the 4 accepted Gospels namely, Gospels of Matthew, Mark, Luke and John.

Other non-Canonical Gospels

Gospel of Marcion, Gospel of Mani, Gospel of Apelles, Gospel of Bardesanes and Gospel of Basilides are all late in origin and are distant to Israel in its origin.

C. A Note on Jesus' Life and Pagan Myths

An accusation that is sometimes levelled against the Gospels' narrative of Jesus' life is that some portions of Jesus' life is very similar to portions of lives of some pagan deities, presumably attempting to discredit the historicity of Jesus, as depicted in the Gospels. A notable similarity that is frequently drawn is related to the death and resurrection of Jesus to some of the other deities such as Osiris, Attis, Dionysus, Mithras, Adonis, Tammuz, Hercules, Romulus, Apollonius of Tyana and Empedocles.

In this context, it is very important to remind ourselves some of our conclusions in Chapters 3, 4 and 5. In Chapter 3, we established that the Gospels, have virtually unparalleled documentary evidence, in comparison to any other ancient historical work. In Chapter 4, we established that the crux of the Gospels, or in other words, the crux of the life of Jesus can be established to be historical by corroborating with extra-Biblical sources. In Chapter 5, we established the logical soundness of the beliefs of the early disciples. In other words, Jesus is a historical person in a historical setting, with beliefs about him among Christians being logically sound.

Reason helps us understand that the conclusions about Jesus are valid and sound regardless of whether someone else, either in fiction or reality, had aspects of his life similar to that of Jesus.

Having said that, just for completeness' sake, it would be worthwhile to point out that, when we get to the details of the lives of the pagan deities, we would find many glaring holes in the argument of similarity with the life of Jesus. For starters, none of these pagan deities is even remotely qualified to be called a historical person. Furthermore, the deaths and resurrections of these deities are in no way like the 'regular' death of Jesus on the cross and a bodily resurrection without unwanted embellishment. Finally, in some cases, it would even be difficult to argue that some elements of the mythologies of these deities even predate Jesus.

THE GOOD NEWS

Introducing the Historical Jesus and His Biographies

Arul Velusamy

Figures

Figure 1 - A Page of Codex Sinaiticus with Text of Matthew 6:4-6:32

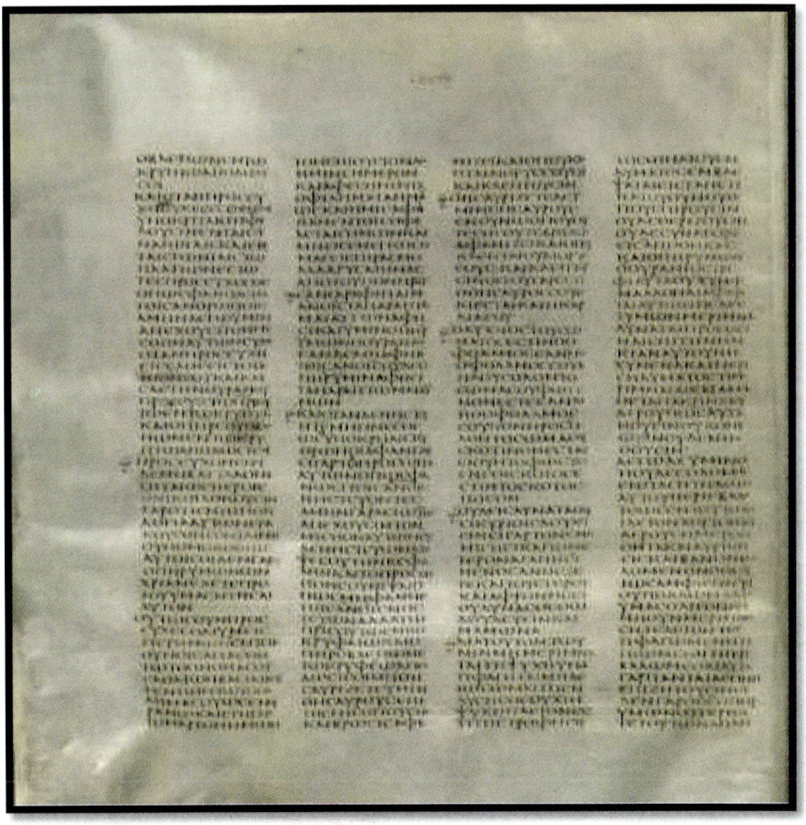

Codex Sinaiticus is a 4th century codex of the Bible (Both the Old Testament and New Testament). The New Testament is near complete (including all 4 Gospels and the Acts of the Apostles).

Figure 2 - A Page of Codex Alexandrinus with Text of the End of the Gospel of Luke

Codex Alexandrinus is a 5th century codex of the Bible (Both the Old Testament and New Testament). Except for 26 leaves of Matthew and 2 leaves of John, the New Testament has text from all 4 Gospels and the Acts of the Apostles.

Figure 3 - Papyrus 104 (P^{104})

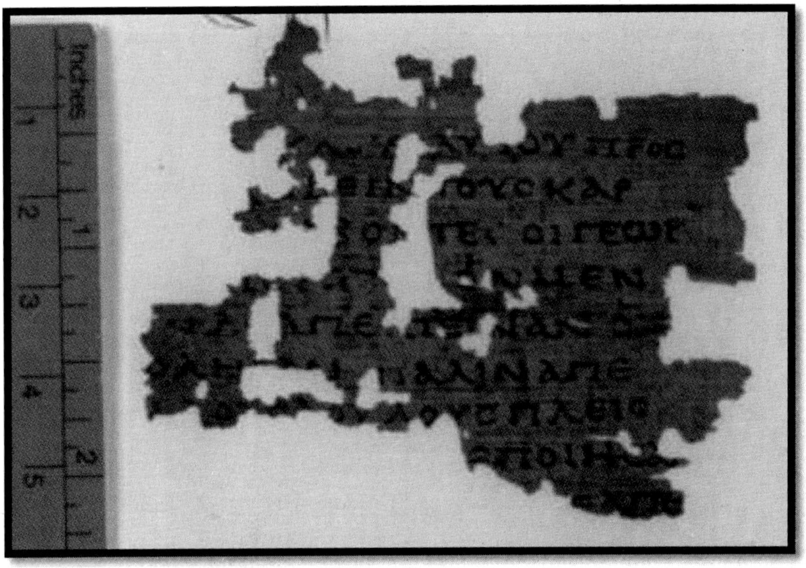

P^{104} has text from Matthew 21:34-21:37; 21:43 and 21:45 and is the earliest of manuscripts found so far for Matthew (AD 150).

Figure 4 - Papyrus 45 (P^{45})

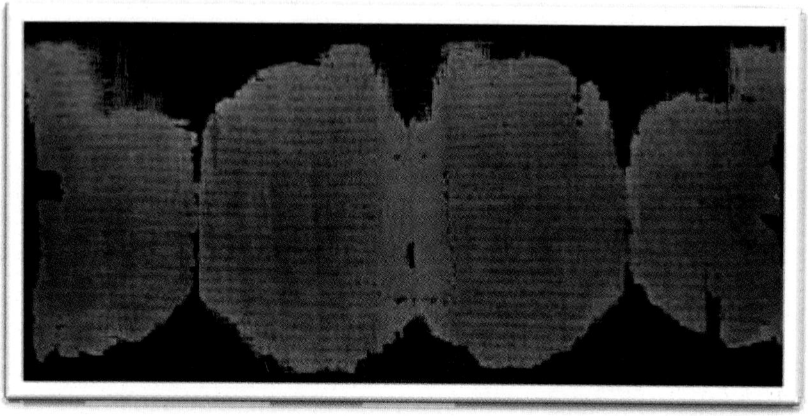

P^{45} has text from Matthew 20-21; Matthew 25-26; Mark 4-9; Mark 11-12; Luke 6-7; Luke 9-14; John 4-5; John 10-11 and Acts 4-17. It is the earliest of manuscripts found so far for the Book of Mark (AD 250).

Figure 5 - Papyrus 75 (P^{75})

P^{75} has text from Luke 3:18-24:53 and John 1-15. It is the earliest of manuscripts found so far for the Book of Luke (AD 175-225).

Figure 6 - Papyrus 52 (P^{52}) - Recto on the Left and Verso on the Right

P^{52} has text from John 18:31-18:33 and John 18:37-18:38. It is the earliest of manuscripts found so far for the Book of John (AD 125).

Figure 7 - A Page of Codex Fuldensis

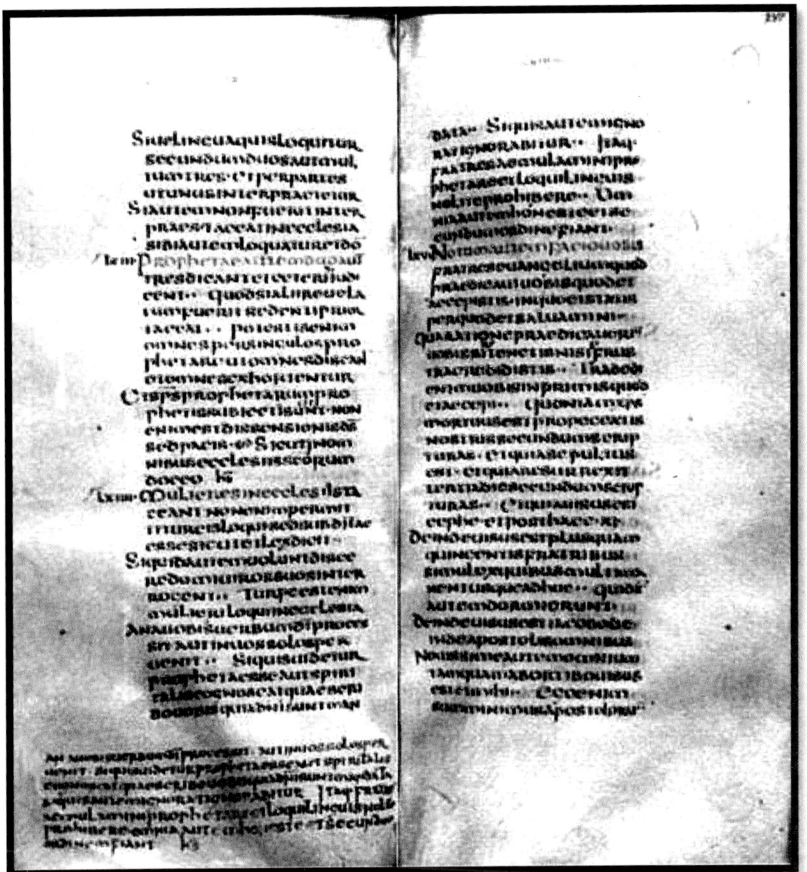

Codex Fuldensis is a New Testament manuscript based on the Latin Vulgate and is dated to AD 541-546.

Figure 8 - Copper Coin of King Herod

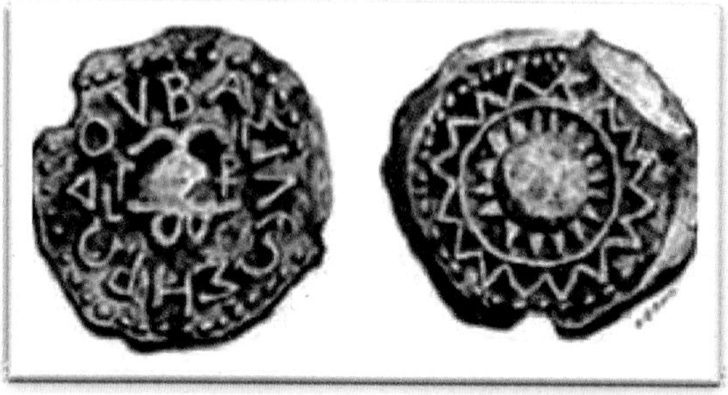

Copper coin of Herod, with the text "ΒΑΣΙΛΕΩΣ ΗΡΩΔΟΥ" (King Herod).

Figure 9 - Coin of Herod Archelaus

Coin of Herod Archelaus, with the text "ΗΡΩΔ ΕΘΝ" (Herod Ethnarch).

Figure 10 - Coin of Herod Antipas

Courtesy: By Classical Numismatic Group, Inc. http://www.cngcoins.com, CC BY-SA 3.0, https://commons.wikimedia.org/w/index.php?curid=2417312

Figure 11 - Coin of Herod Philip

Courtesy: By Classical Numismatic Group, Inc. http://www.cngcoins.com, CC BY-SA 3.0, https://commons.wikimedia.org/w/index.php?curid=2417346

Coin of Herod Philip with the text ΤΕΤΡΆΡΧΌΎ' (Tetrarch) of 'ΦΙΛΙΠΠΌΎ ΤΕΤΡΆΡΧΌΎ' (Philip Tetrarch) visible.

Figure 12 - Augustus Caesar

Courtesy: By Till Niermann - Own work, CC BY-SA 3.0, https://commons.wikimedia.org/w/index.php?curid=388210

Augustus of Prima Porta is a 1st century Roman white marble statue of Augustus Caesar.

Figure 13 - Tiberius Caesar

Courtesy: By Carole Raddato from FRANKFURT, Germany - Tiberius, Romisch-Germanisches Museum, CologneUploaded by Marcus Cyron, CC BY-SA 2.0, https://commons.wikimedia.org/w/index.php?curid=30158434

Figure 14 - Pilate Stone

Courtesy: By BRBurton - Own work, CC0,
https://commons.wikimedia.org/w/index.php?curid=22817908

Pilate Stone is an archaeological artefact found in Caesarea Maritima, Israel, having a 1st century Roman inscription. The inscription records Pontius Pilate along with his official title, Prefect of Judea. The partial inscription reads (missing and conjectural letters in brackets):
[*DIS AUGUSTI*]S TIBERIÉUM [...*PO*]NTIUS PILATUS [...*PRAEF*]ECTUS IUDA[*EA*]E [...*FECIT D*]E[*DICAVIT*]

Figure 15 - A Silver Stater from Corinth, 555–515 BC

Courtesy: By Classical Numismatic Group, Inc. http://www.cngcoins.com, CC BY-SA 3.0, https://commons.wikimedia.org/w/index.php?curid=29087847

The Stater was a Greek silver currency that circulated from the 8th century BC to 50 AD.

Figure 16 - Denarius - A Few Denarii (157 BC Top Left to AD 236 Bottom Right)

Courtesy: CC BY-SA 3.0, https://commons.wikimedia.org/w/index.php?curid=256575

Denarius was a Roman currency which was in use from late 3rd century BC to mid 3rd century AD.

Figure 17 - A Nero Assarion

Courtesy: By Classical Numismatic Group, Inc. http://www.cngcoins.com, CC BY-SA 3.0, https://commons.wikimedia.org/w/index.php?curid=225137

Assarion was a Roman currency (initially bronze and later copper) which was in use from late 3rd century BC to 3rd century AD.

Figure 18 - A Quadrans (= 2 Lepta)

Courtesy: By Classical Numismatic Group, Inc. http://www.cngcoins.com, CC BY-SA 3.0, https://commons.wikimedia.org/w/index.php?curid=504465

Quadrans is a Roman bronze coin which was in use from late 3rd century BC to mid 2nd century.

Figure 19 - A Silver Drachma

Courtesy: By Classical Numismatic Group, Inc. http://www.cngcoins.com, CC BY-SA 3.0, https://commons.wikimedia.org/w/index.php?curid=28979114

Drachma was a Greek currency used from as early as 1100 BC. Modern Drachma also exists.